Burnout to Unstoppable

An Autism Mom's Memoir about Prioritizing Self-Care, Becoming Stress Resilient, and Unleashing Her Inner Badass

by
Claudia Taboada

Health and Wellness Press

Dedication

To *Nico* - for helping me discover the world through your eyes and your exceptional autistic mind. Because of you, I have become a warrior who will not let anyone underestimate your true potential.

To *Alex* - thank you for being responsible, curious, compassionate, and for loving your brother unconditionally. I hope having a mom who realizes her dreams will inspire you to realize yours.

To my mom *Leticia*, who is watching from heaven - thank you for your unmeasurable support through our family's autism journey and for showing me how to persevere in the face of adversity. This book is for you.

CLAUDIA TABOADA

UNSTOPPABLE

SELF-CARE
WORKBOOK

COMPANION WORKBOOK
FOR BURNOUT TO UNSTOPPABLE

DOWNLOAD THE FREE WORKBOOK
To thank you for buying my book, I would like to
give you this thank you gift to *empower* you and
take charge of your life right NOW!

TO DOWNLOAD GO TO
https://www.badassautismmoma.com/selfcareworkbook
OR
send an email to: badassautismmoma@gmail.com

Table of Contents

Introduction

I am the mother of two wonderful boys, Nico and Alex. Nico is on the autism spectrum. After his initial diagnosis at two and a half years old, I had to leave my career as a labor and employment attorney to take care of him full time: researching and learning everything about autism, trying to find the best therapies for early intervention and then homeschooling, fighting for his rights before the health and education ministries, etc. . . . This took a toll on my physical, mental, and emotional health. Amidst the autism whirlwind, I completely *lost* myself.

This book is about my transformational journey from an overwhelmed and burned out mom to an *unstoppable badass*— a disability rights advocate, a multiple marathon finisher, a triathlete, an entrepreneur, an author and a motivational speaker—all while special needs parenting with grace.

This is the story of how I got my life back and how I have used my passion for physical activity as a self-care tool that allows me to manage the chronic stress associated with taking care of my severely autistic son Nico. I hope that my journey will inspire people who are stressed out and overwhelmed, including special needs parents, to realize that self-care (in whatever form) is the foundation to being the best caregiver and person they can be.

I discovered running by accident when we got a service dog for Nico. I started walking with the dog, and in a few months, I began to run. At the time, I had zero aerobic endurance: I could not run for more than two minutes without calling 911! Three months after I started running, I gave myself a present for my birthday and ran my first 5K race. Crossing that finish line would change my life forever. Since then, I haven't looked back. I've run countless half-marathons and twenty-three full marathons around the world, including the six Abbott World Marathon Majors—a challenge I completed by running the Boston Marathon, for which I qualified. I also recently completed IRONMAN 70.3 Mont-Tremblant with very little training but with lots of determination and mental power.

In my case, my self-care tool of choice has been physical activity, particularly running. Running and racing have given me back my sanity and my life. It is the *me* time that enables me to cope with my son's autism diagnosis every day. Physical activity as well as other self-care tools I've discovered along my journey, allow me to be more resilient to stress and empower me to be the best person I can be. Although I apprehend my son's future, I'm no longer paralyzed with fear of the unknown because I know that I will take care of myself whatever this journey may bring.

One of my son's psychologists used to say, "Parenting an autistic child is not a sprint; it's a marathon." I believe that training for and running marathons is a metaphor for parenting a special needs child. It takes patience, dedication, resilience, and perseverance because when that diagnosis hits you in the face, you are *so* overwhelmed that you just feel like giving up but you don't. You can't. It's the marathon of life for which you have to learn how to pace yourself from the outset to avoid early burnout. It's a long-term journey and you need to take all the necessary precautions to reach the finish line alive, including being proactive with your self-care.

Initially, I wrote this book for special needs parents who, like myself, reached a breaking point because they believed that they had to shoulder all the responsibility for the needs of their child, therefore, neglecting themselves. But ultimately, this book is for anyone who may feel overwhelmed by life's events. The message of this book is universal: you cannot pour from an empty cup, and you need to take care of yourself before you can take care of others.

This book is divided into four parts: Part 1 describes how I lost myself in the autism whirlwind and starts with Nico's diagnosis, then the years of early intervention and preschool. Part 2 gives you an overview of the research confirming the dire situation of special needs parents, especially those mothers who, like myself, had to abandon their careers and aspirations to care for their child full time. Part 3 describes how I reclaimed my identity and learned to prioritize self-care. Part 4 describes how I have used running and racing to build a strong mindset and how this has enabled me to go after my dreams and become the *unstoppable badass* that I am today. At the end of most chapters, I give you some insights from my experience as well as some tips to help you deal with similar situations on your own quest for a better you.

My wish is that by the end of this book my journey will inspire you to get your spark back and be the *unstoppable badass* that you are meant to be.

PART 1:
How I Lost Myself in the Autism Whirlwind

Chapter 1: The Beginning

O ur autism journey began on December 19, 2002. Nico was nineteen months old at the time and was this bundle of energy who could not sit still. He was skinny, had big brown eyes, impossibly straight hair, and a smile that could light up a room. He loved to be hugged but not for long as he was always on the move. At the time, I was six months pregnant with my second child and dealing with placenta previa (which causes severe bleeding during pregnancy and delivery). It was a typical Canadian winter: grey, cold, and snowy.

A month prior, my then-husband, Rob, and I had seen Nico's pediatrician for his eighteen-month checkup. We had voiced some concerns about his development to the pediatrician: no eye contact, would not react to his name, he exhibited no joint attention (no pointing at something to bring someone's attention to it, nor looking at something we were looking at). In addition, he had trouble going to sleep every night, had unexplainable tantrums, and was hyperactive. As for his language, it was extremely delayed compared to his peers. At twelve months old, Nico had had a few words like "mama" and "papa," but as time went on, not only did he lose these few words but he didn't seem to be making progress with his language skills.

When I took Nico to a park on a warm August afternoon at fifteen months old, I had my first suspicions that something wasn't right. A mom was sitting on a bench near a sandbox watching her two twin girls play. She invited Nico and I to join them. I took Nico by the hand and asked him if he wanted to play with the girls. He didn't answer but sat down beside them. I sat down beside the mom and we started chatting. When I looked over to the sandbox, Nico was no longer sitting down and for a second my heart skipped a beat. But then I saw him near the slide. Puzzled, I stood up and saw that he was circling the slide, over and over. At first, I just let Nico be and sat back down. Both girls were still in the sandbox, interacting with each other. They came over a couple of times to show something to their mom or point to things in the surroundings. Although they did not have much language, this did not stop the interaction. Once in a while, I looked over to where Nico was still circling the slide. I called him a few times to come and play but to no avail. After fifteen minutes, I said bye to the girls and their mom and went to join Nico. I sat him on a swing and pushed him. As I did this, my mind raced. I was puzzled about Nico's behavior and lack of interaction. My gut feeling was that this behavior was not normal. But given that Nico was our first child, I just thought that he had a little development delay and that everything would be fine soon.

However, on that day at our pediatrician's, my fears were confirmed. She referred us to Montréal's Sainte-Justine Hospital for Nico to be seen at their Developmental Clinic by a multidisciplinary team of specialists ASAP. The word "ASAP" hit me with great force. This was not just a minor developmental delay. My son's condition needed to be evaluated immediately. Suddenly, everything around me became a blur. The doctor kept talking, but I had no idea what she was saying; I couldn't focus and I felt dizzy. I turned to my husband who sat there nodding, looking bewildered.

That day I went home and started what would become my ritual for the next several years—searching the internet for whatever I could find about my son's condition. I began by searching with the words "language delay." However, upon going through several websites and connecting the dots with the other symptoms, I realized that it was not only a language delay but a communication delay, and it was all pointing to the dreaded word: "autism."

When I was making the appointment at the Sainte-Justine Hospital, the secretary had two spots available, one before Christmas and another one in the second week of January. She politely tried to convince me to take the one after Christmas, but Christmas holidays or not, we just *had* to know what was wrong with our child's development.

Nico was seen first by an audiologist, a speech pathologist, an occupational therapist, and then a child psychologist. The diagnosis at the time: "suspicion" of an autism spectrum disorder. Because he was so young (nineteen months), we would have to wait until he was two-and-a-half to have a definitive diagnosis from a child psychiatrist. Then and there, our hearts sank. From my research, I knew that the earlier the autism symptoms could be spotted, the more definitive the autism diagnosis would be. Although I prayed that it was just a problem with his hearing, I *knew* then that my son was autistic and that this suspicion would only be corroborated by the child psychiatrist later.

But there was no time to cry, my first reaction was: what should we do now? Unfortunately, few answers were given to us. A tentative diagnosis was made but no specific treatment was proposed. Just a referral to our local readaptation center to put our name on the waiting list for Applied Behavioral Analysis (ABA) intervention services, the only therapy services that were offered at the time by the public health care system for children on the spectrum. And this is one of the hardest moments a parent of a child with autism goes through in their journey. You are told that your child suffers from a long-term condition which will affect their overall functioning for the rest of their life and all you are given is a paper to register them on a waiting list for public rehabilitation services that may come in a year or two, if your child is lucky.

Obviously, it was a very stressful Christmas. I was in a daze from that point on. A few days after Christmas, Rob and I met with a psychologist at the hospital who had kindly offered to answer some of our questions about autism, the treatments, and services that existed out there, and ultimately, how to cope. I'm still grateful for that offer. But more importantly, I'm grateful to him for being frank and to the point with us. And I still vividly recall his last words: "Be aware that your days of carefree living are over." He was right.

So began the autism whirlwind or rather the autism tornado. First staying up all night doing research on the internet for treatments and therapies, going to the library and reading all types of books related to autism, trying to figure out where to go from here.
As expected, the waiting list for the readaptation center was about a year if not more! This was unacceptable. We needed to act *now*.—

TIPS:
- **Don't feel guilty if you didn't notice the signs of autism earlier.**
- **A diagnosis brings with it many different feelings. Relief, happiness to have an answer, guilt, devastation, grief, fear, anger, overwhelm. Whatever you're feeling is OK, you need to talk about it. Be open with close friends and family.**
- **You need to take care of yourself so you can guide and support your child. Find a therapist who specializes in situations such as yours.**

Claudia Taboada

Chapter 2: Sabbatical

C hristmas came and went, and there was a sense of urgency in our house. With no public services available to Nico for the next year, Rob and I felt the need to do something right away to start working on Nico's communication and cognitive skills, among others.

As most parents of recently diagnosed children with autism would tell you, we felt that we were racing against the clock. The books had led us to believe that if you did not act before your child was five, they would not progress and would never "grow out of their autism."

At the time that Nico was diagnosed, we saw the five-year milestone as insurmountable if we didn't act *immediately*. We believed that if we didn't get our act together right away, our quest to "save Nico from his autism" would be futile. When January came, Rob and I realized the enormity of what lay ahead. Initially, my idea was to take a six-month maternity leave to care for my newborn and enjoy time with Nico before both would go to daycare. But my plans would radically change. I could not envision working full-time in a demanding career such as law (where working part time is not well looked upon), being a mom to a newborn and two-year-old, managing Nico's early intervention program, and dealing with Tom's frequent work travel, among other constraints. Rob and I concluded that, with everything Nico would need, I could not return to work until he had completed his intervention program. We both knew that my career's lack of flexibility meant I would have to set it aside to focus on Nico and the new baby.

I clearly loved my son more than my job; this shouldn't be so hard. But could I do this? "It's the only thing that makes sense," I would tell myself and Rob, trying to be reassuring. "I will be OK. It's just for three years. It's not like I have to give up my whole career."

At first, I saw this as a three-year sabbatical. This was an easier pill to swallow than saying that I was giving up my career altogether. I would take three years off, set up and coordinate Nico's "autism busting early intervention program," and then once Nico was "cured of his autism," I would return to my career. That was the plan. Rob, who is an engineer and had a high management position at the time, would continue to support the family while I took care of the kids and Nico's program. This decision would significantly cut our family income, something that would be a huge stressor, especially that now our expenses would multiply because of Nico's health. To build a well-rounded early intervention team, we had to hire a psychologist, at least two therapists, and possibly other specialists . . . but since "saving Nico from his autism" took precedence over anything else at the time, we didn't really have a choice.

And I truly thought that everything was going to go according to plan. From one of my early searches on the internet after Nico's diagnosis, I remember stumbling upon a book that gave us the exact blueprint of how to proceed. The book was about how after doing a forty-hour per week early intervention program, these two kids were "saved from their autism" by the age of five. Both kids, especially the girl, were engaging in conversations, interacting with their peers, and thriving in preschool. This book became my bible. I would read it every night, underline the important sections in yellow, and put sticky notes where I had steps to follow. Since I had done well in school, I could study and master this too.

After reading this book, I was under the impression that if we were diligent by the time Nico was five, he would be "cured" from his autism, be a social butterfly, and be one of the smartest kids in preschool. Therefore, at that point in time, quitting my career for the opportunity to help my son was a no-brainer: we would work as hard as we could from age two to five and then Nico would "no longer be autistic." As I mentioned previously, I saw this as a three-year sabbatical . . . Boy was I wrong!

TIPS:
- **Children with autism will grow up to become adults with autism. And the wonderful thing is that brain neuroplasticity ensures that children and adults with autism continue to learn until they are well into their adult years.**
- **The works of Dr. Temple Grandin, a US professor with autism, are very helpful and highly recommended.**

Chapter 3: Hospitalized

One day, I was playing with Nico in his room when I felt a sudden pain. I gripped my stomach and breathed heavily. I tried to slow down my breath, but I kept thinking about my baby. What if something was happening to my baby? Each panic thought elevated my heart. I stood up, and just as I did, blood rushed down my legs. Seeing the blood, I sobbed and stumbled to the kitchen to grab my phone. Rob took me to the ER, and I didn't come home for three weeks. Thankfully, my mom, who lived in Ottawa, was able to come to Montréal and take care of Nico while Rob went to work. Even as I lay in my hospital bed, I focused on Nico's program. I made an appointment for Nico with one of the only behavioral psychologists in Montréal. I also called the psychology departments at all the local universities to find students who could work with Nico regularly. After interviewing a few students from my hospital bed—I wouldn't be slowed down. I was on a mission—we chose five. I then began to search for a behavioral psychologist. I was amassing an army to fight off autism.

A tower of books about autism sat atop my swivel table. I empowered myself with knowledge. Early intervention, communication, the benefits of occupational therapy, play and autism . . . I was determined that when I returned home, I would establish the early intervention program of our dreams.

Soon after I went home, two more bouts of bleeding landed me back in the hospital, and when I was full-on hemorrhaging, doctors told me I couldn't go home at all until my baby was born. I was devastated not to be able to be with Nico at such an important time. I wanted to hold him and help him any way I could. I wasn't concerned with the blood pouring out of me like a faucet. My son needed me.

One morning the bleeding wouldn't stop and they wheeled me in for a C-section. Alex was a feisty ball of energy. Contrary to Nico, he had no trouble with nursing. In two days, we returned home. Our family had grown. It was joyful and exciting to welcome Alex home, but the stress and anxiety still permeated our days.

During my hospital stay, I felt sort of in control: I was plotting, planning, putting the theoretical pieces of a road map to "save" Nico together. I couldn't wait to get back home and start executing the plan. However, it wasn't until I got back home after Alex was born that I realized the enormity of the task at hand. This was it. This would be our life for at least the next three years. From now on, not a single second would go by without me thinking about Nico's diagnosis.

TIPS:
- **Set boundaries and make sure to take care of yourself from the outset of the journey.**
- **Always check in with yourself and make sure that you remember that you exist. Breathe.**

Chapter 4: Operation Intervention and Definitive Diagnosis

So, as soon as I got back from the hospital with Alex, I got back to work on getting that early intervention program off the ground. It was early April 2003, and Nico was approaching his second birthday. And yes, I was feeling anxious and overwhelmed, but I was also feeling hopeful for the future given Nico's young age. I started searching the web like crazy for any information and trainings about autism that I could find locally. I needed to feel competent in this new autism adventure. I had a new role as head chief of operations, and I wanted to master it. First on the list was deciding which specialists needed to be consulted to ensure that Nico would have a well-rounded and multidisciplinary early intervention program. This was necessary because when dealing with an autism diagnosis, all aspects of development are affected, including but not limited to motor skills, language and communication skills, play skills, behavioral skills, etc.

The first specialist that needed to be on the team was the behavioral psychologist in charge of the overall early intervention program. From word of mouth and my research with the Québec Board of Psychologists, we narrowed down our search to a couple of psychologists and chose Dr. Martin. She was very knowledgeable in the field of behavioral analysis, was very patient, and had a very calm demeanor.

We also chose the two therapists who would be working with Nico under Dr. Martin's supervision. We invited the psychology students I had chosen to the house for a second interview and more importantly to interact with Nico. I wanted to see their attitude and disposition as they played with Nico. Would they be scared? Intimidated? Cheerful? Relaxed? . . . By the end of the interview process, we selected two students: Brenda and Guylaine. Both had different personalities: Brenda seemed quieter but efficient, while Guylaine was more of an extrovert and seemed very playful. Around Nico they both seemed in control, gentle, and patient.

I went to my first autism conference. I would leave no stone unturned. The focus was on ABA intervention. This was the method that my autism bible book recommended but also the only approach that was backed by research at the time. In recent years, the aims and methods of ABA therapy have been questioned by a fiercely articulate and vocal community of adults with autism, many of them childhood recipients of ABA. Because, at the time, we didn't know of any other therapies, ABA would be the basis of our early intervention program. After the conference, I was even more convinced that we were on the right track. Three years. Check all the boxes. Do all the things. I could handle this. After I got home and put the kids to bed that night, I put all the conference materials in a binder, reread the important parts, and made a summary of what to do next. I would be prepared and knowledgeable for the meeting with Dr. Martin which was the next item on the never-ending to-do list.

So, the two therapists, Rob, Nico, and I met at the office of Dr. Martin. Dr. Martin explained the essence of the early intervention program, gave us an overview of the skills that would be taught as well as the way that notes and results would be compiled. Because Nico was so young at the time, the first skills to be taught were basic skills that we usually take for granted in neurotypical children such as attention, imitation, making requests for desired items, motor skills, etc.

The next item on the agenda was to set up the therapy room and buy all the necessary props for the lessons prescribed by Dr. Martin. Indeed, there were so many things we needed—toys associated with the intervention program such as plastic animals, cartoon characters in all sizes and shapes, puzzles and blocks, fine and gross motor activity materials and props, sensory reinforcers, etc.—that we needed a separate room dedicated to the therapy sessions. We decided that our dining room would become the therapy room; therefore, we needed some extra shelves to store all the necessary props, our autism book collection (which was already becoming quite large), and Nico's toys.

My mom, who had been temporarily living with us during my hospital emergencies, had to go back to Ottawa for a knee operation, so I figured that I needed to be very efficient with my time before she left. I wanted to make sure that the setup for the therapy room was on point and that most of the important errands related to the early intervention program setup were done. I was still nursing Alex, so my mom would come with Nico and me to do our shopping for furniture and props. She would care for Nico while I would go off someplace quiet and nurse Alex. We went to Ikea to buy furniture, like a small table and chairs, and to the Dollar store to get sensory toys like stretchy strings, squishy balls, and fidget toys to be used as reinforcers.

As Nico was about to turn two years old, it was now becoming increasingly important to obtain a definitive diagnosis to have a stronger position when negotiating for government services. We also needed to know where in the spectrum Nico would lie to modify the home early intervention program if necessary. Dr. Martin would have to decide if after the diagnosis, she would need to add or tweak some programs.

When Nico received his tentative diagnosis, the developmental pediatrician referred him to a child psychiatrist at Montréal's Douglas Hospital. In April, we received a call from the Douglas Hospital's Autism Clinic to come in with Nico for an evaluation and a more definitive diagnosis by one of their child psychiatrists.

The autism spectrum is very large. Indeed, the symptoms and characteristics of autism can present themselves in a wide variety of combinations, from mild to severe.

Web MD states that "Autism spectrum disorders include social, communication, and behavioral challenges. These problems can be mild, severe, or somewhere in between." Until recently, experts talked about different types of autism: Asperger's Syndrome/High-Functioning Autism, Pervasive Developmental Disorder Not Otherwise Specified (PDD-NOS), and Classic Autism. Now they are all called "autism spectrum disorders."[1]

On the milder side of the spectrum, there is Asperger's Syndrome, which is often confused with High-Functioning Autism. Both have the same type of symptoms with the difference being those with High-Functioning Autism have a language delay and those with Asperger's don't. Highly intelligent, both are very functional and autonomous in their daily life. They may also be really focused on topics that interest them and discuss them non-stop. Socially, they can be awkward and very anxious. In the middle of the spectrum, we have the PDD-NOS diagnosis which encompasses those children and adults who are more severe than Asperger's and High-Functioning Autism but less severe than those who have Classic Autism.

Classic Autism is defined by Medic 8 "as the most serious form of autistic spectrum disorder."[2] It is also known as "severe autism." Someone with classic autism has noticeable problems with speech, behavior, and social interactions. They are also extremely sensitive to any form of sensory input such as touch, sounds, smell, and sight. They may also be nonverbal or their speech may be severely impaired to the extent that they cannot articulate words and sentences and may have to rely upon other forms of communication. They also may be more withdrawn than people with the other types of autism and may avoid contact with other people.

The day of Nico's diagnosis was a blur.

It was a multidisciplinary affair where, apart from the child psychiatrist, Nico would be evaluated by a speech pathologist and an occupational therapist. As Rob and I spoke with the psychiatrist, both the occupational therapist and the speech pathologist interacted with Nico. The occupational therapist had a big container with sensory toys (squishy balls, shiny objects, and strings) and another one with dry beans and lentils (to put his hands in and feel them to get much-needed sensory input). Nico found a pink squishy ball with plastic spikes that he liked and began to jump up and down. But as the occupational therapist tried to sit Nico on the swing they had in the room, Nico began to have a huge tantrum. Kicking, flailing his arms, screaming. Both the occupational therapist and the speech pathologist tried to calm Nico down to no avail. Rob and I stood up and turned around. "I'll take care of it, keep talking," I told Rob. I was trying hard not to cry. I felt powerless. Mortified by this scene and feeling self-conscious even though these therapists were probably used to worse, I held Nico in my arms tightly for about five minutes. As he started to calm down, the occupational therapist gave him the pink squishy ball. I slowly stood up, gave Nico a reassuring squeeze, and a peck on the head and went back to the conversation with the psychiatrist. Our worst fears were confirmed: Classic Autism. He tried to be reassuring but nothing could prepare me for these words. I had a knot in my throat and felt out of breath and stabbed in the heart. I looked over at Rob who looked equally *demolished* by the news.

Although I knew that the definitive diagnosis of autism was coming, I was hoping that this was going to be just a language delay or a motor delay of some sort. But the psychiatrist confirmed that the three spheres of development that usually affect people with autism were affected. More specifically, Nico was exhibiting: (1) trouble with social interaction (2) impaired communication (3) restricted interests and repetitive behaviors.[3] He also advised us that according to his evaluation, Nico had an intellectual disability and because of this, we should not expect him to reach the intelligence of a child older than seven or eight.

The car ride home was torture. Rob and I were silent . . . and *devastated*. My head was spinning and I felt sick to my stomach. Even though on the outside, I seemed to have accepted our fate by being extremely diligent in setting up the early intervention program, my secret hope was that all this would just be a terrible mistake. In my dreams, I imagined the child psychiatrist just ripping up the Sainte-Justine tentative diagnosis and telling us that Nico would miss some milestones, but that in two or three years, he would catch up and be just like the other neurotypical kids.

In the evening after I put the kids to bed, I told Rob that I needed to go to the pharmacy but instead I drove around to ugly cry in the dark. And I cursed at the Universe: Why our son? Why our family? Why me? . . . I was heartbroken but I had to soldier on. Time was of the essence and we needed to keep up with our program because "we were going to beat this diagnosis" no matter what, or so I thought.

TIPS:
- **A diagnosis is always a shock, even if you have been expecting it. Definitely take it seriously but don't let it consume or paralyze you. Instead, let it spur you into action.**

- **Although the diagnosis may tell you to lower your expectations of your child, *do not settle. Ever.* Always set high expectations for your child. Because your child may surprise you when you least expect it.**

On May 10, Nico's second birthday, we had a quiet but memorable celebration with our closest family members. By this time, everyone knew that Nico had been diagnosed, and they were very much understanding of the situation. They could now attribute his autism to most of the unexplainable tantrums he would have at family gatherings, including the huge one that he had at my sister-in-law's when he heard the kitchen fan for the first time. They could also now better understand Nico's total lack of interest in playing with his cousins. It was actually another huge load taken off our shoulders as we did not have to pretend or explain any of Nico's behaviors to the family anymore.

TIPS:

- **Once you have a diagnosis, do not hesitate to tell family and friends; it will put everything into context and you may get more help and understanding.**
- **Family and friends who love you will usually be very understanding of the situation.**
- **Even if they don't offer to help you, at least they are now aware that your child's behavior is the result of a medical condition rather than your lack of discipline.**

In the days before my mom left, the prep continued. I bought binders, notebooks, pens, and paper for the therapists and made photocopies of the different score sheets that were needed for each of Nico's programs. I had also borrowed a few psychology books from Dr. Martin's library. I remember skimming through those books after the kids would go to bed, hungry to learn as much as I could about what we were about to put Nico through. I would select the sections in those books that I wanted to photocopy and run off to Business Depot. My mom would stay with the kids. I would then grab a coffee at Tim Horton's. This little ritual lasted no more than three–four days, and without realizing it, this was a little bit of a self-care moment—the only one I had available to me at the time. And one that would no longer be available when my mom left.

There was a huge void when my mom went back to Ottawa. Not having her to help me care for the kids was one thing but the hardest part was not having her there to hold my hand during one of the most difficult periods of my life. Since I'm not one to show my feelings, I wanted to act, not cry. But my mom knew exactly what I was going through without uttering a single word. And hand-holding she did plenty as she provided the emotional support she was so good at giving. My mom would come and visit us in Montréal every four months and would stay two or three weeks at a time. Because of my hospital scare with Alex, she stayed over three months this time around.

My mom's support on our family's autism journey was unmeasurable. After Rob, she was the only person in whom I confided my pain, my fears, and my hopelessness. After particularly harrowing days where I tried to hold things together for the sake of the kids, she would hug me or just hold my hand. Other times, while I was furiously doing my autism research on the internet after the kids went to bed, she would come to my home office and bring me tea and a warm blanket. She would also make sure that I ate properly and that I didn't skip meals. It dawned on me that now I was going to be alone for most of the day taking care of a newborn, my autistic child, and managing an early intervention program. Rob would try to come back home early but the work never stopped. It was quite the load, but I thought that I could handle it, physically and mentally. I had no idea what was coming next.

TIPS:

- As the saying goes: "You cannot pour from an empty cup." You have to take care of yourself before you can take care of others. I for one made the mistake of not doing so.
- Go for a walk, go for a coffee, go to the mall to do some shopping alone or with friends or your significant other but *leave* the house! It is *essential* to your mental health. Do it now. Don't wait.

Chapter 5: Working the Program

We blew out Nico's birthday candles and started therapy. Dr. Martin came to our house to observe the student therapists, Guylaine and Brenda, work with Nico. First, she showed them how to run the sessions and then she observed and made suggestions. The therapists worked on seven programs simultaneously, including imitation, gross and fine motor skills, attention, etc. They would repeat the same drills over and over until Nico mastered them.

Guylaine and Brenda each worked with Nico ten hours every week, two hours each morning and each afternoon from Monday to Friday. The program called for forty hours a week of early intervention work, but since we were not receiving any type of funding by the government at the time and only had one salary, we could not afford to pay for more therapist hours. Instead, in addition to orchestrating everything, I took on the role of Nico's "generalization therapist."

I worked around the clock, making sure that *every* interaction with him outside of his therapy hours was "a learning moment" and that whatever he learned in therapy, he was generalizing (transferring what is learned in one setting or situation to another without explicitly teaching it) to other contexts. Generalization is a huge problem for people on the autism spectrum.[4] For example, if a child learns how to tie his shoes with his mother at home, we presume that he will naturally be able to tie his shoes in the presence of his teacher or on his own in the preschool setting. In typical development, generalization is a given. In autism, those generalization skills need to be taught. So, as the generalization therapist, I made sure that whatever skills Nico was learning, he was transferring into other contexts at home, the park, the mall, the grocery store, etc. It was exhausting but again, I thought I could handle it, even with a newborn who also needed my full attention.

One day I was in the kitchen preparing lunch and Alex was in his playpen beside the kitchen. Nico had just finished his morning therapy session and was watching a video. The phone rang and I was relieved to hear the friendly voice of my former coworker and lawyer friend, Marie-Pierre. I had missed her since I left work. She wanted to hear my news as she had been on vacation when I left for maternity leave, and we hadn't had a chance to catch up. She had heard the rumor that I wouldn't be coming back to work.

Marie-Pierre and I had become fast friends the year prior, as we had been working long hours doing research for a pharmaceutical class action suit. She had grown up with an older sister who had Down syndrome. As we poured over law books, she used to tell me stories about how proud she was of her sister and the fact that she was going to a vocational school where she was learning how to cook and how to work in a cafeteria. It turned out that this vocational school was not only attended by adults with Down syndrome but also by adults with autism.

We also talked about her worries about having children. As a special needs sibling, she had found that part of her life very challenging. Marie-Pierre told me that she loved her sister with all her heart, and was afraid of the burden she was becoming to her aging parents as she was not independent and needed constant supervision. The caring for a special needs person was, as Marie-Pierre put it that day: "*tout un contrat à vie*," a lifetime contract. At the time, I had my fears for Nico's development but never in a million years had I thought I would be in her mother's shoes.

"Nico has been diagnosed with autism and I'm not going back to work for now," I said in no uncertain terms.

"Oh my God, Claudia! How are you taking this? I am so sorry. How is Nico? . . . and the baby? I cannot begin to imagine how you have managed to handle all of this," she said, her voice almost cracking.

"Don't worry, Marie-Pierre, everything is under control. We have an incredible psychologist and two therapists. Besides, Nico is only two years old, and all the autism books are telling us that if we start intervention now, he may be cured of his autism when he is five. So, I expect to be going back to work in about three years. It's really only a sabbatical."

But Marie-Pierre knew full well what kind of life was ahead of us, especially for Alex. I reassured her repeatedly that things were under control and spoke of the checked-off boxes, the hired help, the program in place. Then Nico started screaming and flailing, pounding the table. Alex flinched, looking scared, and started to cry. "Hold on," I said as I put the phone down. I rubbed Nico's back as I tried to calm Alex. They both got louder, and I needed to stir the food on the stove. "Hold on, Marie-Pierre," I told her over to the phone. "I'll call you back. Sorry," I said abruptly as I turned off the stove.

I felt guilty that we had to end our conversation this way and of all the people I did not want to turn off from having children, Marie-Pierre was probably my number one on the list. I was worried this episode would leave a bad taste in her mouth—after all, she was so hesitant to have kids. Above all, I wanted to tell her that no matter the chaos and the uncertainty that was ahead of us, we would get through it . . . but the reality is that I wasn't so sure.

And for the first year of Alex's life, this was our reality. Aside from taking care of my newborn, my newly diagnosed autistic child, and the house chores, I was managing our home program, juggling the schedules of the therapists, and driving to all the appointments with other therapists and doctors. This was on top of doing research at night and reading as much as I could on autism. But the toughest job of all was being Nico's generalization therapist. I felt I had to do it all and be Nico's hero on top of it all. The pressure was dizzying.

TIPS:
- **For the longest time, I appeared like this superwoman under control, but I was not. Don't tell people you have things under control. You don't. That's OK. Say that you don't know what the *f**k* you are doing.**
- **People will probably lend a hand more freely. Ask for help.**

Chapter 6: Building a Village

Nico's first year of therapy came and went in a flash. I never had a moment to pause, reflect, or even be completely present with Alex. Before Nico's diagnosis, I was looking forward to taking some time off after Alex's birth, maybe four months, maybe six. I had wanted to fully enjoy this precious bonding time with Alex and take both boys to the Botanical Gardens, the Biodome, the municipal pool, without pressure without stress. But this was not to be.

Alex and I could rarely have precious bonding time, as I was *always* busy thinking about Nico and ways to "save him." Even while I nursed Alex, I was always thinking about what to do next with Nico. I could not even go to the park alone with Alex without feeling stressed and anxious. I felt like I was neglecting my second child because the first one was monopolizing all my time and more. This is probably one of the worst and most harrowing feelings a mother of a special needs child can have. Feeling incompetent and inept toward the children who don't have a condition. The guilt was overwhelming. I couldn't be present with Alex, and I knew it. I was spreading myself too thin and things had to change.

TIPS:

- **Siblings of special needs kids need their moms too. Do not make the mistake of spreading yourself so thin to the point that you have no more energy left for your neurotypical children.**
- **Try to have one-on-one time with them, even if it's just to go for an ice cream cone around the corner.**

Unfortunately, apart from my mom who lived in Ottawa, there was not much help around us in the form of family and friends. My mother-in-law would help us once in a while when I had to go to a conference or when Rob and I would have meetings with specialists sans Nico, but she no longer had the strength to care for Nico and Alex regularly. Most of my friends had careers, worked full-time, and had kids and responsibilities of their own. Rob would try to come home early, but I could not count on him, as sometimes he had last-minute meetings that would go all afternoon and evening. Worse, his company was based in the UK, and sometimes he had no choice but to leave me alone because of business-related travel.

So, I decided to look for some outside help during the day, someone who could help me care for Alex a bit and do some light housework while I was busy with Nico. I remember contacting a couple of agencies and putting an ad in the newspaper. After three interviews, we selected Aurélie who had recently immigrated to Canada from France. Aurélie was about twenty-five years old and was gentle and warm. And although she didn't know much about autism, she bonded right away with Nico and Alex. She saved us. And while this would have an impact on our already strapped budget, it would be one of the best decisions we ever made.

Aurélie came five days a week for two to three hours and would care for Alex while I went to appointments with Nico. She did some light housework and laundry. You would not believe what a source of comfort and relief this was. With Tom's frequent travel, it was reassuring to have someone at home just in case I had to go see the specialists or doctors with Nico. But most importantly, having someone I trusted take Alex to the park while Nico was having a tantrum or while I was busy speaking to Nico's therapists was worth millions. It was a huge stress reliever. Aurélie took care of Alex until he was eighteen months old and old enough to attend full-time daycare. She was definitely an invaluable player in our autism journey, and I will forever be grateful to her.

TIPS:

- **It takes a village, and if you don't have a village, make one.**
- **Hire someone. Contact autism organizations that can help you find assistance.**
- **Reach out to other special needs parents to see if you can exchange babysitting duties.**
- **It's about your wellbeing as a person and a parent. You need help. Get it.**

Chapter 7: Comparison

At around the time we hired Aurélie, Nico and I began a two-month autism program designed to give parents tips on how to interact and encourage communication and play with their kids at the Douglas Hospital in Montréal. A psychologist was in charge along with a speech pathologist, an occupational therapist, and two educators. Since the program would be held for two months only, we decided to try it. Before signing up, we met with Dr. Martin to ensure that whatever we were going to do with Nico in the program did not contradict our early intervention program at home. We got the green light. For two months, we dropped the morning session and kept the afternoon therapy ABA session only. The focus of this afternoon session would be mostly play and imitation to give Nico a break.

The Douglas Hospital program was run like a daycare: they started with circle time, then a small snack, group exercises led by the occupational therapist, another snack, some arts and crafts, and then individual sessions with the speech pathologists. I saw it as a great opportunity to learn new ways to stimulate Nico. It was also the first time I met other autism parents—some of whom I still keep in touch with. The group was made up of children with different severities of autism. Some kids were already very verbal, other kids were nonverbal or had just a few one-word sentences. Some kids would have tantrums, others would be very hyperactive. There was quite a range of behaviors.

Here, I realized that Nico's type of autism was middle to severe. Of course, we already had the definitive diagnosis of Classic Autism handed to us by the child psychiatrist, but deep inside, I refused to believe it or at least I was hopeful that what was said in the diagnostic report was only temporary and that soon Nico would be showing signs of "recovery." But as I started comparing him with the other children in the group, I began to get worried.

I remember one particular incident that happened at circle time. All the children started gathering in a circle with their parents sitting behind them. As everyone was quietly sitting, Nico let out a scream and dropped to the floor. He began crying loudly, flailing his arms, and kicking. I tried to calm him down, but he kept kicking and screaming. A parent gratefully handed me a fidget spinner and I tried to put it in Nico's hand, but he was so agitated that he just threw it. I felt the stares from the other parents and finally an educator helped me carry Nico outside of the class were I eventually calmed him down by rocking him back and forth. Nico stopped crying but was still upset. I was sobbing. I felt helpless. I felt anxious. I was beginning to question my hope for Nico's future.

I remember comparing Nico to the other more verbal and more functional kids in the group, and it broke my heart. I would watch the other kids progressing rapidly and sitting and focusing for longer periods than Nico. Other nonverbal or less verbal kids who said only a few words at the beginning of the program were now chatting away as if they had no expressive language delay . . . and I felt *jealous* that despite everything we were doing, Nico wasn't making much progress either with his attention, speech, and gross or fine motor skills. He continued to have huge tantrums at circle time and, even though the other parents were extremely understanding, *I felt the stares*.

TIPS:

- Do not *ever* compare your child with autism with another child with autism.
- As Dr. Stephen Shore said, "If you have met one person with autism, you've met one person with autism."[5] This means that no child with autism is the same. The autism spectrum is very large and each child has strengths and limitations that vary according to the degree of their autism.
- For me, this was and continues to be a struggle. It is easy for me to say that to preserve our sanity, it is best to stop comparing. In reality, it pains me to say that I still do it. And yes, it is destructive and detrimental to our mental health, but it is part of human nature. However, as our children grow older, we forget to measure their progress by the missed milestones. Rather we embrace their different abilities and begin to measure their progress in those spheres in which they have talents and strengths.

Chapter 8: Breakthrough

When the program was done, we promptly resumed the morning early intervention sessions. The two therapists were back at it, working morning and afternoon with Nico while I continued the generalization work outside of the therapy sessions. The work was relentless for us all, but the superhero was Nico. He worked tirelessly, harder than anyone of us. His only break was a forty-five-minute nap after lunch.

After about seven months of therapy and all the effort and work from everyone involved, Rob and I were getting a little antsy and I realized that we were not seeing much progress with our ABA home program. We attributed this to the fact that Nico was only doing twenty hours a week with the therapists when he should have been doing forty. We felt guilty that we could not afford to pay for the other therapy hours and we were starting to get pretty discouraged and anxious for Nico's future. We were also getting pretty stressed out by the fact that bills were piling up and we were seeing very limited progress.

But then there was a breakthrough. One that parents of neurotypical children take for granted. For neurotypical children, imitation comes naturally. It is a given that they will imitate their caregivers first and then their peers. A baby and mom's early back-and-forth imitation of each other's sounds, actions, and facial expressions is really a conversation without words that is a precursor to communication and language as well as social interaction. Unfortunately, children with autism often have great difficulty with imitation. And this struggle with imitation often has a negative impact in other areas of development such as language, play skills, interaction, and joint attention (the ability to share a focus with another person on an object).[6] Some autism experts may argue that imitation is the precursor for everything. Imitation is so intrinsically linked to so many developmental milestones that it is a key component of autism intervention. And it was definitely key to Nico's home early intervention program.

The problem was that Nico was not responding. One day, Alex was with Aurélie at the park, and I decided to look more closely at the imitation session Brenda was doing with Nico. They were both sitting down face to face on the Ikea chairs. Besides her, Brenda had her notetaking binder as well as the container with all the props in duplicate. For the first task, she instructed Nico to tap the table with his hand. After ensuring that Nico was looking at her, Brenda said, "Nico fais ça" and she tapped the table. Nico did not respond. He looked distracted and agitated. Then Brenda asked Nico to clap his hands. Once again, Nico did not respond. Putting maracas in front of him, she tried getting him to shake them while she shook hers. At this point, I thought that the maracas' noise would help Nico focus better. But no. Once again, Nico did not respond. I could feel Brenda's discouragement, and as she looked over at me, I gave her thumbs up sign and told her to keep going. Deep inside, I was extremely concerned and desperate for a breakthrough. Nico had trouble focusing. It was a mixture of brain immaturity, lack of attention, being distracted by other sensory stimuli, etc. I was worried; the team was worried. The Imitation Program is one of the cornerstones of ABA, and if Nico could not master this first, then the rest of the pyramid would be shaky.

But then one day, Nico surprised us all. On the week leading up to this big breakthrough, I had bought a videotape of the TV characters the Backyardigans. Nico loved this one song—I don't remember the exact name of the song but if I remember correctly, it was a song where the characters would sing and point to their body parts. Every time that this song would come on, our hyperactive Nico would stop in his tracks and be utterly transfixed by the TV. One day, I decided to use this video as a teachable moment. I crouched behind Nico and I took his little hand, modeled the pointer finger, and as the video played, I started pointing to Nico's body parts with his own pointer finger. We did this a few times on two separate occasions. Then the next time, I crouched beside Nico and I imitated the characters myself, trying to get Nico to do it. He didn't, and I didn't push him. I just continued crouching behind him and doing the pointing from behind.

Then magic happened! A few days later, Nico started doing all the drills at the table with Brenda. She would clap, he would clap. She would tap the table with one hand, Nico would do the same. She would play with different toy instruments like a small piano, maracas, a toy flute, and Nico would follow. I had gone out to a meeting with our social worker at the local readaptation center. Alex was with Aurélie at the park. When I came back from my meeting, Brenda was almost in tears—tears of joy! She was in the middle of another program but she almost screamed at me to come over to the therapy room. Nico was still sitting on his little Ikea chair, and he must have been amused at Brenda's antics. Brenda reached for the plastic container with all the imitation props and asked Nico to copy her actions.

And as if Nico had been touched by a magic wand, he began to repeat all the movements Brenda was asking him to do, one by one. Then, to see if these skills would be replicated with another person, Brenda asked me to sit down in her place and do what she had done. And lo and behold, Nico imitated every single action I did with the props and with my body. Then after a quick discussion with Brenda, I added a few actions with my hands that were not in the lessons (like touching my nose, knocking on the table, scratching my knee, etc.). Nico followed each of those to a T! The most important thing of all was that Nico was having fun. His eyes were focused and his body was following every single one of our actions. Brenda and I were overjoyed and both took turns hugging and kissing Nico. He was also due for a cookies and chocolate milk snack after all his efforts!

While Nico was having his snack, Brenda called Dr. Martin. She told her everything that was happening, and I could hear Dr. Martin in the background just screaming with excitement. She suggested that we stop other lessons for the day and focus on solidifying Nico's emerging imitation skills. She asked that Brenda and I continue to take turns and ask Nico to follow us around and do new imitation tasks around the house and backyard to see if Nico could generalize these imitation skills to other settings. We would be doing the same with Guylaine and then ask Rob in the evening to do some more generalization of his own. The theory behind this was that if Nico ended up doing this, then it meant the Imitation Program was mastered, and we could move on to other programs.

So, as soon as Brenda hung up, we began to strategize. I went into Nico's room and the washroom and asked him to imitate me doing different tasks like reading a book, opening and closing his drawer, brushing his teeth, etc. Brenda went to the playroom and backyard and asked Nico to imitate gross motor movements like jumping on the trampoline, running, throwing a ball, etc. Nico did it! He felt proud every time we cheered for him. Although he rarely made eye contact, he would look at us every time we clapped or gave him a high five. He imitated *everything* from life skills to fine motor and gross motor skills like brushing his teeth or jumping on the trampoline. We were stoked and so was Nico! He kept it up with both Guylaine and I in the afternoon and with Rob in the evening. To see if the Imitation Program was mastered, we needed to follow the strict ABA mastery criteria which were to obtain 80-100% success in two consecutive sessions with two different instructors in random rotation. Well, on that fateful day when Nico discovered imitation, all the criteria were mastered *at once*!

I felt ecstatic. I was overwhelmed with excitement, and most importantly, incredibly proud of my boy, my superhero. *These* were the moments that made all the effort, the stress, the anxiety worth it. Having abandoned my career and my aspirations to help Nico, these moments gave me the validation and the encouragement needed to keep going. So, during those first three years, we began celebrating triumphs many would regard as small, but, which for us, were *huge*. Unfortunately, it was a long wait until the next one.

TIPS:
- **As Dr. Temple Grandin has so accurately stated, "Keep *focusing on strengths rather than deficits* in children with autism."[7]**
- **Don't freak out about the missed milestones or lack of progress. Often, parents get so concerned about their child's deficits that they don't focus on their strengths. Children with autism continue to *progress at their own rhythm* and that is OK. Build on what your child is good at, whatever that is.**

Chapter 9: Words!

Nico was approaching three-and-a-half, and we were still waiting for progress in receptive and expressive language. Early in the process, we had decided that French would be Nico's primary language at home. This would avoid mixing Nico up with English and further delay his language. So, we requested that the therapists and other people in Nico's entourage only speak French to him. Despite this precaution, Nico's language and communication skills were not improving.

We then decided to add a new therapy to the mix. We had heard of a certain Dr. Roberts and how his program was changing the lives of some autistic children in Montréal. Rob and I were curious, so I made an appointment to see him as soon as he had availability. We met Dr. Roberts with Nico in tow, and after some brief testing, Nico was accepted into his program.

We were to begin the therapy sessions as soon as possible. Because I was the main generalization therapist at home, we decided that it would be best if Rob did this short program with Nico to avoid any conflict between therapies. However, four months into this therapy, Dr. Roberts realized that Tom's travel was hindering consistency. So, he suggested that I take over because it would be easier to track progress, and I was with Nico all the time already helping him to generalize his other skills. I was so used to adding responsibilities that I automatically agreed. So, I began this new quest to get Nico to acquire language, avidly learning from Dr. Roberts.

TIPS:
- **Learn to say *no*! It is not easy when you have a child with a long-term condition and you feel like you are racing against the clock.**
- **It is not easy when you feel guilty that you are not exploring all the therapies that are supposed to help.**
- **But sometimes, you have to delegate.**

About six months into this program, Nico began to make some progress in his receptive and expressive language skills. I still remember the first time Nico said one of his first spontaneous words. Nico had just finished his morning session with Brenda and I sat him and Alex down to watch some TV while I prepared some lunch. I gave both boys a plastic cup of juice while they waited. As I was chatting away with Aurélie who was about to leave, I felt Nico tug at my pants. He had his little plastic cup in his hands. Since I was still talking to Aurélie, I didn't really pay attention. Nico tug at my pants once again, but this time he was actually uttering a word: "*jus*"! And he even extended his little arm to hand me the cup. Aurélie and I looked at each other and we almost had tears in our eyes! I picked Nico up and showered him with kisses. Alex who overheard all the commotion came in and joined the celebration. I picked Alex up as well and planted a big kiss on his cheek. We couldn't wait till Rob arrived to share the good news!

Apart from juice, Nico's first spontaneous words were milk, cookies, toast, cereal, pizza . . . words that were used to request his primary need to eat and drink. Eventually, he would expand his repertoire to request leisure activities like music, video, trampoline, book. Of course, this breakthrough in language is one that parents of neurotypical children take for granted. But not us. Even though Nico was at least two years behind his neurotypical peers, this was a huge accomplishment and we felt blessed. Nico was expressing his needs and wants and that's all that mattered. This decreased the number of unexplained tantrums. My baby could say what he wanted and get it! This progress gave me the strength to keep going. It was another wonderful period in our journey when I felt extremely proud of my Nico. This validated our collective efforts and justified my own sacrifices. I felt proud of our family. And I felt proud of myself for staying the course despite the early challenges.

We were really excited about Nico's language progress with this method, and, as I did with all previous therapies, I invested myself one hundred percent in learning everything about it. Taking notes and asking questions, following Dr. Roberts's recommendations to a T. Again, I bought all the things and made every moment a teaching moment, rain or shine. We also incorporated other aspects of this therapy (like working on self-regulation) into regular activities like walking, going to the park, going grocery shopping, or going to the mall. The objective was to help Nico use breathing to calm his sensory system when the sensory stimulation around him got too intense.

So, Nico would work two hours with Brenda in the morning, two hours with Guylaine in the afternoon, and then sometime in the evening, usually right before dinner, Nico and I would do our language lesson. And we kept this up for almost three years.

Eventually, however, Nico hit a plateau in his language progress. Although at the table sessions, he was able to make two- and three-word sentences, he didn't generalize this skill outside of the table and apply it in our daily life, either with me, Rob, the therapists, or anyone else. Occasionally, he would string two or three words together, but this attempt would be the result of us using direct prompts (like asking him what he wanted). Spontaneous communication was not happening and we were beginning to get worried.

After discussion with both Dr. Martin and Dr. Roberts, we decided to get rid of all forms of direct prompting and focus on getting Nico to speak longer sentences by using only indirect prompts (like showing Nico the object of his affection and waiting for several minutes until he would make the long-awaited sentence). And that's what we did, day in and day out. The therapists would work on spontaneous language during their sessions by using sensory toys and fun games that Nico could repeatedly request.

I would try to work on spontaneous language during the day, using meal times where Nico could request his favorite foods and drinks, only giving him a tiny bit of food or drink to make him ask again. Like the therapists, I kept a written log where I would record all the communication attempts and words Nico said each day. This written log had several columns. But the key column was the one where we would record the language that was completely spontaneous—without any sort of prompt whatsoever. By the end of the week, I would compare notes with the therapists and make adjustments.

Again, at the beginning of this quest for spontaneous language, we saw an increase in longer sentences "*je veux faire dodo*," "*je veux boire du jus*," "*je veux manger biscuit*, ("I want to sleep," "I want to drink juice," "I want to eat a cookie"). But shortly we realized that Nico was only requesting the things that were specifically taught either at the table with the therapists or with me during meal times or during the day. In other words, Nico wasn't generalizing and wasn't making any spontaneous requests.

What we didn't really grasp at the time is that for expressive language to expand to sentences and back-and-forth conversation, speech must be preceded by gains in communication. Communication includes many nonverbal cues that are essential for interacting and communicating with others, such as gestures and facial expressions. Because of Nico's very limited communication skills, we had to go back to the drawing board and determine how we could best support Nico in this continuing quest to expand his language.

TIPS:

- **In the whirlwind that is autism intervention, there will be obstacles and the need to change direction at times. It is OK. It is part of the journey. Don't despair.**
- **Ideally, you want to stay consistent with the same program and add other programs as the need manifests.**
- **If you hit a roadblock, find alternative ways to crack the code. And keep plowing through.**
- **Keep the eye on the prize—which is, in my case, a happy autistic child, adolescent, and adult who would develop his unique talents and abilities and thrive despite his limitations.**

Chapter 10: Adding to the Mix

A s I mentioned previously, the ABA method was the only intervention that was backed by research at the time and we went with it because, frankly, we didn't know any better. When we felt that progress in both receptive and expressive language was not materializing, we added Dr. Roberts's therapy to work on expanding language as well as self-regulation. Dr. Roberts's therapy was also based on behavioral modification. Even with this new addition, Nico's language skills were stalling, and we realized that there was more to autism than behavior modification.

By spring 2005, Nico was approaching his fourth birthday. He was now a little older and wiser, always with a mischievous grin on his face and his curiosity showing through his big brown eyes. He still had trouble sitting still for long periods of time and was still very sensitive to sounds and other sensory stimulations. Although Nico had made some strides with his two therapies, the specter of preschool was hovering above us. We felt that we needed to add another therapy (or two) to the mix to address some deficits that were not being addressed by behavior modification alone.

Back when we had done the two-month program at the Douglas Hospital in the fall of 2003, we were provided two reports: one from the speech pathologist (with different exercises to help

Nico develop his communication skills) and another from the occupational therapist (giving us exercises to develop Nico's gross and fine motor skills and, most importantly, to work on his sensory integration issues). At the time, we had reviewed these reports but had put them aside, as we blindly trusted our ABA program. However, the more time passed, the more we felt that we had to add these two therapies to work on additional skills that were not fully covered by ABA. So, we decided to add speech pathology and occupational therapy to the mix.

We first contacted a speech pathologist who had been referred to us by another autism parent. Speech-language pathologists are the professionals who assess and diagnose people with deficits in speech, language, and communication. For the first year or two of Nico's early intervention program, we, like most parents, didn't really understand the differences between language skills and communication skills. Language skills include the ability to understand others (receptive language) and the ability to express oneself (expressive language). Communication skills pertain to the nonverbal cues we use to share and interact with others (like eye contact, facial expressions, gestures, pointing to show and share, etc.).

Communication skills are a precursor to language skills.[8] Just think of how neurotypical babies and toddlers are able to communicate with their caregivers without uttering a single word. They smile, nod, make eye contact, point with their index finger, give objects to share without saying words or sentences. Because of this early communication and sharing, these babies and toddlers understand early on that communication is a two-way street. As they age, they go on to say words, make sentences, and eventually hold conversations.

Unfortunately, in autism, these early communication skills and nonverbal cues are rarely present.[9] These have to be specifically taught prior to or along with language acquisition in order for language skills to develop easily and to be generalized to other contexts.

Next, we found an occupational therapist, also through word of mouth. In autism, occupational therapists help with kids' sensory integration and their inability to filter out sensory stimulation (from lights to sounds to touch, etc.). This not only wreaks havoc with their focus and attention but sometimes, it can become so overwhelming that it can cause pain, oftentimes resulting in aggressive and/or self-injurious behavior. Through different protocols, occupational therapists work with autistic children and adults on reducing their sensory hypersensitivities. By doing so, people with autism become more present, can better focus on the tasks at hand, and become less scared and/or aggressive when their senses are overwhelmed.

So, we hired both specialists and Nico began sessions twice a month with each on an alternating basis. Both the speech pathologist and the occupational therapist would interact and work with Nico while I observed. Then they would write a short report for me with recommendations to try at home.

So, I became Nico's de facto speech pathologist and occupational therapist, trying to replicate at home what I was learning at every appointment. This, of course, was in addition to all the work I was doing to generalize the skills worked on in the ABA program and Dr. Roberts's program.

And yes, wearing different hats at the same time was exhausting, but I was so desperate to save my child that I didn't notice. I was going through the motions and praying that all these therapies would somehow magically work together in tandem to help Nico "get out of his autism." Because this was the key to all the sacrifice; all the sleepless nights; and all the blood, sweat, and tears: "saving Nico from his autism before the age of five." I saw this as a battle that we were going to win.

And for the next year, in addition to his ABA home program and my language sessions based on Dr. Roberts's method, Nico saw the speech therapist and the occupational therapist twice a month with the objective to help Nico prepare for preschool. We wanted to help Nico improve on different skills: language and communication, gross and fine motor, play, and pre-academic skills while helping him tolerate sensory input.

TIPS:
- **If language is not happening with your child, contact a *speech therapist* to verify if there are any missing communication precursors. A speech therapist can also tell you if there is a problem with apraxia of speech (an oral motor condition in which children have difficulty connecting speech messages from the brain to the mouth) in which case augmentative and alternative communication devices can be used to facilitate speech.**
- **If your child has trouble filtering sensory input, consult an *occupational therapist* who can help with reducing hypersensitivities and increase focus.**

Chapter 11: Rock Bottom

Nico's fifth birthday was quickly approaching and "D Day" was almost here. It was the day that we all had been working toward for close to three years. Psychologists, specialists, and therapists were all on board. The plan was to have Nico attend a regular preschool without informing the principal at the outset about his autism to gauge if Nico's autistic behaviors would be perceptible by the personnel and other children and whether Nico was academically ready to start following a regular curriculum for his age.

Although we felt some hesitation, Dr. Roberts convinced us that this was the right thing to do. Not only that, apparently this was a strategy used by many parents wanting to see if progress had been made in their early intervention programs. After all, we, especially Nico, had put in hard work and sacrifice. We all believed Nico would come out of his shell, demonstrating his potential, and showing everyone that he had "been cured of his autism," just like in the book that had become my bible. This was Nico's marathon. Nico had worked hard and relentlessly for three years. He had learned; he had been coached for hours on end about how to behave and how to adopt neurotypical behaviors so he would seem "normal." It had taken patience and perseverance from all concerned. Here we were—Nico's time to shine! Soon, he would make friends and thrive in preschool. I would be able to resume my career, and our family life would become normal again. According to Dr. Roberts, Nico was just raring to go and ready for this new turning point in his life, or so we thought.

In early February 2006, I had found a private preschool about a twenty-minute drive from our house. I had done some research on the internet about the preschool, the principal, the curriculum and read all the reviews, which were mostly positive. I knew from their website that if we paid their monthly fee (which was quite steep), they were open to accepting new students at different times of the year. So, I called to see if Nico could start in April. Of course, I did not mention that Nico had autism. I told a white lie—that he may have some language delay because we spoke three languages at our house (English, French, and occasionally some Spanish). The principal was very gracious on the phone and proposed that in two weeks, Nico come in for a tryout from nine to noon. He would have the opportunity to do circle time, the calendar, some academic activities, have a snack with the others, and then do more fun activities.

So, the stage was set. Nico would begin at this preschool the last week of April. We had about two months to prepare Nico for this moment of truth. Everyone was working extra hard, especially Nico. We had to make sure that all the spheres of his development were covered: speech and communication, play, motor skills, academics, behavior. Outside of his therapy hours, I would take him to the mall and the grocery store to practice self-regulation. We would also work on motor skills at the park. We would go and practice skipping, throwing, and kicking a ball. I would try to organize play dates to gauge where Nico's social skills were at. If it was exhausting for me, imagine how exhausting this was for Nico, especially since we were trying to turn him into someone he was not and *someone he did not really need to be.*

One thing that the speech pathologist recommended to prepare Nico was to use a social story. A social story is an individualized short story that breaks down a challenging social situation into understandable steps.[10] So, I made sure that I prepared a social story with pictures and short sentences to explain to Nico what to expect at the preschool in terms of behaviors. I would read it to Nico every night for two weeks with the hope that he would understand that some behaviors were not tolerated by the teacher (like standing up and running around). I also made sure that at least a few days prior, we drove around the area where the preschool was located. I would excitedly point to the school and tell Nico that this is where he was going to meet some new friends, learn all about the letters and numbers, do arts and crafts, sing songs, etc.

So, the end of April arrived. Nico's preschool tryout or "D Day" was just around the corner. The day prior, I made sure that Nico had a quiet day to be physically and mentally ready. I suspended all therapies for the day and made sure Nico would be rested. We also went for a haircut and shopping for some nice spring clothes. We had some lunch and then sat on a bench at the park. After having Nico's favorite mango ice cream, I read to him the social story for the umpteenth time. I still vividly remember that moment. Nico was looking at me intently and he smiled a few times. I sensed that he probably felt my urgency and he wanted to reassure me and ease my fears. And fearful I was. Very. Would Nico understand the rules? Would he remain seated while the teacher taught her class? Would Nico have a tantrum at circle time? I realize now that all the while, I was secretly hoping that Nico would be an exemplary student.

"D Day" was upon us. It was Wednesday, April 26, 2006. I still remember that day as if it were yesterday. Sitting at the kitchen table, I anxiously ran my finger along the rim of my coffee mug. I had asked Rob to take Alex to daycare so I would not rush Nico this particular morning. Nico trotted down the stairs with bright eyes. 7:30 a.m., a good night's sleep. I took a deep breath. Go time. His gluten-free cookies and his caramel pudding were waiting dutifully in his lunch bag. We had breakfast and went upstairs to choose the clothes he would wear for this special occasion. I said, "Nico, which shirt do you prefer? The one with Elmo or the one with Big Bird?" Nico pointed at the one with Big Bird. When he finished dressing up, we brushed our teeth together and then it was time to go.

It was a gloriously warm morning. I brought with me the social story to read one last time. The preschool started at 9 a.m., and I wanted to arrive near the preschool at least half an hour early so we could take a short walk around, find a bench, and read. I parked the car and we went for a leisurely walk to be at the preschool by nine. I was nervous but Nico seemed unfazed. We found a good spot, and I read the story to Nico one last time, really putting an emphasis on what a fun experience he was going to have and all the friends he was going to make at this wonderful school.

After our little walk, we made it to the preschool. Nico was holding my hand and looked interested in what was going on. I held on to Nico until the principal came to meet us. She was chatty and said hi to Nico with a big smile. She encouraged me to bring Nico to his class and speak to the teacher at the same time in case I had anything I wanted to discuss with her. So, we went into this bright and beautiful classroom, all painted in pastel tones and with huge and colorful circle-time carpet. As soon as the teacher saw Nico, she knelt beside him and said excitedly, "*Bonjour, Nicolas! Es tu prêt pour t'amuser et apprendre?*" (Hi, Nicolas! Are you ready to have fun and learn?). I kept holding Nico's hand as if I was afraid to let go of him in this noisy labyrinth of sensory stimulation. I held on while I spoke to the teacher for a couple of minutes.

I didn't say a word about his autism. I only mentioned to her that Nico was very shy and that he had a language delay because at home we spoke three languages. That was it. Was I setting my child up for failure? You bet. Did I have any other choice? Perhaps, but now it was too late. All I could do now was to pray that Nico's "neurotypical skills would come through" and that he could "perform" to the best of his abilities. I eventually let go of Nico's hand, knelt beside him, and gave him a peck on the cheek wishing him good luck. To the teacher, I may have seemed composed, but on the inside, I couldn't have been more apprehensive and anxious. I stood by the door for a fraction of a second and said bye to Nico, with a mixture of guilt (for leaving him alone and "throwing him to the wolves" so to speak) and anticipation (feeling hopeful that Nico would actually enjoy this new experience). I don't think Nico noticed me leave as he was already busy looking and running around the classroom.

Once I left the preschool, I looked for a café nearby so I could wait for Nico and be available for any calls from the principal. I had given her my phone number in case she or the teacher had any questions about Nico's routine. I found a Starbucks around fifteen minutes away, ordered a large latté, a scone, and waited. At the time, I had just discovered a new therapy called Padovan (or Neurofunctional Reorganization) which seeks to rehabilitate the nervous system by re-creating the evolutionary movement patterns that lead to brain maturation. I had been at a workshop on the Padovan method three weeks prior, so I had brought with me all my notes to reread again and organize them by relevance. I was completely absorbed by the task at hand when the phone rang. Not even an hour had gone by. I honestly thought that the principal and teacher wanted to know more about Nico and which activities he liked to do more at home or something to that effect. But *I was wrong*.

The principal sounded serious, almost harsh—the opposite of her outgoing demeanor an hour earlier. She told me in no uncertain terms that I had to come and pick up Nico *immediately*. The teacher told her that Nico was not only disturbing the class, but he would not focus or pay attention to anything she was saying and teaching. During circle time, Nico didn't want to sit with his classmates. Instead he ran around and played with a slinky he found in one of the toy boxes. He also played with the curtains and some strings he found on the floor. Nico didn't want to sit for arts and crafts either, and when he did sit, he made a mess by throwing the hand paint all over the table. Now the kids were about to have their snack and I just needed to come and get Nico ASAP! My heart sank. Suddenly, I felt out of breath, almost dizzy. I had a lump in my throat. I so wanted this to work for Nico, for our family, for me, but it was not to be . . .

I promptly gathered all my stuff. Threw out my half-full cup of latté, had a bite of my scone, and off I went to get Nico. When I arrived, Nico was already at the principal's office, the kids in the class were already eating their snacks. Nico was calmly sitting down and had *his lunch bag with him unopened,* meaning that he had not even been allowed by the teacher to sit with the other kids and have his snack, meaning that the principal did not even have the courtesy to allow my boy to have his snack in her office.

The principal gave me a lecture. She asked me if I had noticed if my son was different and had some weird behaviors like running around aimlessly, jumping up and down and flapping his arms and hands, looking at things on the side, and lining up objects. She said that she and the teacher had noticed that not only did Nico have an attention problem but that he may be on the autism spectrum. Of course, I knew all of this, but I couldn't tell her that! I just acted as if this was news to me and told her that yes, I had noticed that Nico was a little hyperactive but nothing out of the ordinary. I also told her that I was grateful for her observations and feedback. She gave me a few names of schools where Nico's behaviors could be accepted and where he could learn at his pace. She also told me to have Nico tested for both autism and attention deficit hyperactivity disorder (ADHD).

I thanked the principal for the opportunity she gave Nico and for all the helpful information and tips she had given me. I took Nico by the hand and left. Nico and I walked toward our car silently, *with Nico still carrying his unopened lunch box*. I could not even ask Nico how his experience was, as Nico was still mostly nonverbal and nonconversational. He seemed like the same happy go lucky boy he was when I dropped him off, and that made me even madder...Yes, I was *mad, stunned, resigned* and *plain sad*. And that unopened lunch box would become a symbol for *intolerance, narrow-mindedness*, and *discrimination* against invisible disabilities and . . . one which I vowed to fight against for the rest of my life.

As I sat in the car with my boy eating his snack, I felt guilty. I felt defeated. I felt like all the sacrifices we had made had been for nothing. I started crying and cursing at everyone, including God: "Why Nico? Why our family? Why me? Why bring someone into the world to suffer like this? Why on earth send this child into this world to have intolerant people treat him like he was some kind of freak?"

I stayed in the car for well over a half an hour crying my eyes out. Nico was just eating his snack, probably very aware of what was going on. For a flicker of a second, I thought that life would be easier for everyone if I just went into the garage, put on the exhaust, and then just let it be. I was ready to go and bring my boy with me. This was no world for him to be living in. Full of people who did not care to understand him, people who did not care to adapt to his needs, people who were plain disrespectful of differences. I realized that no matter what effort we were putting in, Nico would not come out of his autism by the age of five, contrary to what we had been led to believe by the literature at the time. Nico did not deserve to be treated like this by this teacher, this principal, or anybody else for that matter.

I calmed down and decided to bring Nico to the park where I had read the social story—which now I just wanted to shred to pieces. We played a little on the slides and the swings and then we went to McDonald's where I bought Nico some chicken fingers and a small bag of fries. I kept my sunglasses on to hide my puffy eyes.

I was going through the motions like a zombie. I would like to think that Nico was oblivious to my pain, but we will never know. We went back home because Nico had a therapy session with Guylaine. Once we arrived, I asked Nico if he wanted to have a nap, but he didn't. So, we went outside to the backyard and we played with the ball a little bit. Then we watered the plants with the hose together and Nico started to jump up and down from excitement and flapping his arms.

I sensed that Nico wanted to play with the water. Since it was a beautifully warm day, I helped Nico put on his bathing suit and I set up the water hose. Nico was in his element, so carefree, so cheerful and insouciant. I stared at him for a few seconds, went to the side of the house where no one, not even Nico could see me, and started crying again—but this time, the floodgates were wide open. I crouched and held on to my knees in a fetal position rocking back and forth and I kept crying inconsolably. How long did I stay there? I don't know. All I know is that at that time, I also had a thought for myself.

Yes, *me*, Claudia Taboada, the person who had been absorbed in this autism whirlwind and didn't know who she was anymore. I felt sorry, *so sorry for myself*. Sorry for having sacrificed my career and my life for this illusion that "we were going to cure Nico's autism by the time he was five years old." This is when my three-year sabbatical was supposed to end so I could go back to my career and pursue my life aspirations. But, of course, it was not to be. I knew deep inside that going back to work and having my life back was no longer an immediate possibility. *There was still so much to do.*

Once there were no more tears left, I got up, checked to see if Nico was still playing with the hose. And he was. Just having a blast like a typical boy his age. And when I saw that smile, I began to cry again but this time, my tears were of *defiance*. Looking at that smile made me shift my mindset. I promised myself and Nico that I would continue to do everything in my power to help him, no matter the obstacles. This child needed his parents to be completely behind him, and I *could not abandon the fight*. I needed to keep going for him. And as I was saying this, I also knew full well that *I would keep forgetting myself in the process*. I would keep basing my self-worth on Nico's successes and setbacks. I would keep living my life on autopilot. I would keep forgetting about my appearance, not even having the energy to comb my hair. I would keep eating the same thing over and over for convenience and forget to drink water regularly. I would keep forgetting to schedule coffee or workout dates with my friends to clear my head. I would keep going to bed late reading about autism, even though Nico would sometimes wake up at all hours of the night. I would keep forgetting to schedule *my own* doctor's appointments. Essentially, I didn't exist anymore. I was a shadow of my former self. At this point, I had completely *lost my identity*. And yet, I still vowed to plow ahead and continue to help my boy.

I waited for another few minutes and then we went inside. Not sure to what extent Nico noticed or understood why mommy had a red nose and watery eyes, I just gave him a peck on the cheek, held him tightly for a few minutes, and then we went upstairs. Nico needed to put on some dry clothes and have a snack before Guylaine arrived. I needed to wash my face. We resumed our daily routine.

TIPS:
- **If I were going to start that preschool experience all over again, I would not only be transparent with the autism diagnosis from the outset but I would offer the principal and the teacher all of the support necessary to make this a positive experience for everyone involved, especially Nico.**
- **The supports are the following: (1) having a "shadow," an aide to accompany Nico in an inclusive classroom in order to be a support to him by either assisting with skills already mastered in a therapy**

setting or by helping with the acquisition of new skills,[11] (2) asking what kind of physical adaptations can be made to the environment in order to decrease Nico's sensory load, such as dimming the lights, making the classroom less noisy by lowering the noise coming from the air conditioning vents, creating a smaller class size, etc. (3) offer autism support to the teacher (including a psychologist, a speech pathologist, an occupational therapist or other professionals as needed). With the ultimate goal of eventually fading out the need for the shadow and allowing Nico to function on his own.

One unexpected and positive outcome from this experience was the realization that apart from his autism, Nico could probably be suffering from some kind of attention disorder that could be hampering his learning as well as his social skills.

Chapter 12: A New Ordeal

Next, it was back to the drawing board for Team Nico. Everyone acknowledged that Nico's lack of ability to focus was a huge factor hampering both his academic learning and his social skills. So, we needed to deal with the attention issue as Nico's time to attend a public school classroom was fast approaching. We decided to apply to the school board for a one-year deferral to have more time to work on Nico's attention, academics, and social skills, and we got it. We needed to figure out if Nico's lack of attention was due to his sensory issues, to another underlying attention problem, or to both.

I had mentioned to the psychologists and to both the speech pathologist and the occupational therapist that the preschool principal had suggested that Nico be screened for ADHD. And everyone agreed that this should be the next step in our journey, as such a condition could have symptoms affecting how the current therapies and interventions were working. Therefore, we needed to identify any new diagnosis and treat it separately from Nico's autism.

The scientific research in autism states that nearly three-quarters of children with autism also have other medical or psychiatric conditions.[12] This is called "comorbidity," and the conditions are often called "comorbid conditions." Comorbid conditions can appear at any time during a child's development. Some might not appear until later in adolescence or adulthood. These are the most common comorbid conditions that might be diagnosed in children with autism: anxiety, ADHD, clinical depression, seizures and epilepsy, motor difficulties, intellectual disabilities, and developmental delays.

ADHD and autism can have very similar symptoms. Children with either condition can have difficulty focusing. They can also be impulsive and have trouble in school. Their lack of attention and focus can affect their social skills and relationships. According to Web MD: "Though both autism and ADHD share many of the same symptoms, the two are distinct conditions. Autism is a series of related developmental disorders that can affect language skills, behavior, social interactions, and the ability to learn. ADHD impacts the way the brain grows and develops. And you can have both."[13]

In Nico's case, it was not obvious to pinpoint where exactly this lack of attention and focus came from. So, I contacted Nico's pediatrician to have an appointment with a child psychiatrist who would be able to make this distinction. After some research, our pediatrician came up with a name: Dr. Eric Fombonne from the Autism Clinic at the Montréal's Children's Hospital. We met with Dr. Fombonne, a child psychiatrist and world-renowned epidemiologist, in the fall of 2006.

Nico was to begin school in September 2007, so we still had a full year to adapt the early intervention program and all the other therapies in case Nico was diagnosed with ADHD. I don't even remember what kind of tests Dr. Fombonne performed on Nico that day. All I know is that by the end of the appointment, he had concluded that Nico was both autistic *and* had ADHD. He also mentioned to us the possibility of giving Nico medication to reduce both his hyperactivity and impulsivity. This was the first time we had heard of medication to deal with some of Nico's symptoms, and, of course, we were scared. We had heard so many stories of children having serious side effects after taking medication that we decided to think about this seriously and do our own research before deciding what to do.

With this ADHD diagnosis in hand, we went back to Team Nico to determine how to help Nico better focus on the tasks at hand and avoid distractions. One thing was certain—Rob and I were wary of medication and wanted to avoid giving it to Nico, if not absolutely necessary. We would only back down from this position if the conclusion from all concerned was that Nico's lack of attention and hyperactivity could no longer be contained despite the modifications to our comprehensive early intervention program. Three months after our appointment with Dr. Fombonne, we decided to try medication. If we wanted to help Nico progress on the academic front, the language and communication spheres, and his social skills, we needed to nip the ADHD in the bud. And that could only be done with medication.

Thus began the quest to find Nico's perfect ADHD medication (as well as the right dosage). It was a quest that took us a few months, with mixed results and a lot of suffering and stress for everyone concerned, especially for Nico. First, we tried Ritalin for about three months. Thankfully, there were no side effects, but there were no real positive results either. Then we tried Adderall. For the first couple of weeks, we didn't see any effects, good or bad, but gradually, a different Nico emerged. A Nico who seemed more grounded and more attentive to his surroundings.

Out of therapy, he was able to sit down for longer periods of time while doing tasks like arts and crafts and playing games on the computer or watching TV. While we were out and about for walks, at the park, the grocery store, or the shopping mall, Nico seemed less impulsive and would stay by my side without me having to run around to get him or scream his name to come back. The therapists also noticed that Nico was more attentive during the therapy sessions. The academic tasks that were very hard for him to focus on, such as handwriting, were suddenly easier for him, and he began to do more complex puzzles and be more motivated while doing fine motor tasks, like coloring, beading, and playing with playdough. Adderall seemed to be doing the trick and, most importantly, seemed to be side effect free—until it wasn't.

Three weeks after we began to see positive effects, Nico began to cry uncontrollably in the late afternoon, just before dinner time. He would just be in his room or the TV room and he would suddenly cry and engage in self-harm, something he hasn't done since he was three years old. Self-injury is one of the most devastating behaviors exhibited by people with autism and developmental disabilities. The most common forms of these behaviors include head-banging, hand-biting, and scratching.[14]

One day, I was preparing dinner in the kitchen when Nico screamed loudly. I almost dropped the mixing bowl I had just pulled out of the cupboard and raced up the stairs. He was in his bedroom just waking up from a short afternoon nap. As I entered his room, I saw him hit his head against the wall. I jumped, immediately grabbed him, and forcefully held him. He was kicking and flailing his arms. He wanted or *needed* to go back to that wall and hit his head. We stayed like this for over twenty minutes. Nico was shaking. I was shaking. It was obvious that Nico was in pain, probably a headache. But since Nico was mainly nonverbal, he could not express or explain where this pain was coming from. When the pain seemed to subside, he stopped kicking and flailing his arms. His screams turned to sobs, and eventually, he calmed down. After he relaxed his body like a rag doll, I helped him lie down on the bed. His eyes were open and they were filled with tears. He was as scared as I was, *and he could not tell me what just happened.* It was heart-wrenching. Lying down beside him, I stroke his head. I felt utterly helpless, tears coming down my cheeks.

These episodes would last for a few weeks and they would always happen at around the same time. I would hold him to console him but also to prevent his self-injurious behavior. I kept trying to ask him what he was feeling both verbally and by using pictograms and pictures of boys crying and holding their head, but I got no response. I didn't know what to do other than to stay with him until the pain went away. I felt powerless, unable to protect my boy. Where the heck was this pain coming from? Nico had a brief period of head-banging when he was three. At the time, we had been so worried that we went to see a neurologist. The neurologist had Nico pass an EEG and tested him for epilepsy. At the time, it was concluded that Nico didn't have epilepsy, but the neurologist asked us to continue to be on the lookout for any type of head-banging behavior and any other more traditional signs of epilepsy such as staring spells, uncontrollable jerking movements of the arms and legs, loss of consciousness or awareness, etc.[15] Eventually, that self-injurious behavior stopped suddenly just as it had appeared.

Could these new head-banging episodes be related to epilepsy? We began to observe Nico more closely during the day. I asked both therapists to record any unprovoked crying, head-banging, and staring spells. After observing for a few days, we concluded that he had no traditional epilepsy-related symptoms. We also observed that the head-banging always happened around the same time: in the early evening—between five and seven. We decided to continue our observations and I contacted Nico's pediatrician for an urgent appointment.

Two days later, we were at the pediatrician. She examined him first and then we talked. I described Nico's behavior in detail and showed her the log we had been keeping with the therapists—no staring spells, no loss of consciousness or awareness, and no jerking movements. We recorded only sudden uncontrollable crying and head-banging between five and seven p.m. She knew that Ritalin had given inconclusive results and that now we were trying Adderall . . . Suddenly, we both had a light bulb moment: Could this head-banging be an Adderall side effect?

The timing of these episodes was definitely suspect, as they had started about three weeks after Nico had his first Adderall pill. According to Nico's pediatrician, these were not epilepsy symptoms but he was obviously having some head pain, and his head-banging probably sought to relieve some of the symptoms. She decided to give me a recommendation for a neurologist. However, because of the long waiting list, we would also be considering the hypothesis that this could be an Adderall side effect. We would continue with the current dosage of Adderall for the next couple of weeks, and if the pain did not subside, we would start reducing the dosage to see if things would improve.

So, for the next couple of weeks, we decided to stay the course and observe. It broke my heart that we couldn't do anything for Nico immediately and get rid of this pain permanently. But at the same time, I believed then that we were probably on the right track and just needed to trust Nico's pediatrician. The same pattern continued. After two weeks, I called the pediatrician and we agreed to cut the Adderall dosage in half for a couple of weeks, then try to fade it out completely after. Eventually, it would take another month before the pain subsided and the head-banging episodes stopped.

Nico was back to his old hyperactive self, but at least he was no longer in pain. We stopped the medication tryouts for the time being. Eventually, when Nico was older, we tried Risperdal (for sensory stimulation-related anxiety), Vyvanse, and Strattera (for hyperactivity and attention). More medication tryouts were necessary but none with the horrible side effects we experienced during that time. To this day, Nico takes Risperdal and Strattera, and we continue to monitor their side effects by having Nico take a blood test every six months. The side effects of these medications are related to water retention, weight gain, and hormonal imbalances.

TIPS:

- If you find it is worth it to try medication, do so under the advice of a doctor you trust.
- Keep a detailed log of behavior change and side-effects. Find out what to look for and make all caregivers aware of the possibilities.

Chapter 13: Asleep at the Wheel

So regardless of the medication ordeal, Team Nico kept going. We were undeterred and continued with the program for the next year. By this time, one of the therapists, Guylaine, had been accepted to do her masters at a university outside Montréal. Instead of replacing her, our psychologist and I decided that since I was already doing my table session with Nico as well as doing the generalization of skills, I could become his therapist and focus mostly on academics.

The lifelong learner in me welcomed this opportunity, as it allowed me to do research on how to adapt the regular preschool curriculum to Nico's autism and ADHD needs. I prepared the lessons, taught them, and helped him generalize these skills—adding more responsibilities to my already loaded schedule. But again, I didn't even think twice. All I wanted to do was to help Nico and best prepare him for school.

No time to think about myself really, just staying the course as our psychologist would always say. As I was completely immersed in the autism whirlwind, I didn't have time to drink coffee with friends, workout, get a haircut, get my nails done, shop for new clothes . . . it had been so long since I had thought about having time for myself that adding a few responsibilities wouldn't make a difference to my everyday life, my happiness, or my worth . . . or so I thought.

So began this new stage of intervention, heavily focused on language, communication, self-help skills, and of course, academics. Brenda would be working on the first three spheres in the morning and I would be working on academics in the afternoon and continue incorporating in our daily routine whatever new skills Nico was learning with Brenda, the speech pathologists, and occupational therapists. Obviously, we could see the contrast between a more focused and attentive Nico (while taking Adderall) versus a Nico without medication who was back to his old hyperactive and impulsive self. But there was not even a question of going back to Adderall. We had to adapt our styles of teaching to this reality.

We trusted that our psychologists and both of our specialists, especially our occupational therapist, would figure out ways to help Nico be less distracted by all the sensory stimulation around him. So, during this time, we relied heavily on occupational therapy as well as physical activity to help Nico become more grounded and be more receptive to learning. The occupational therapist, who, up to this point, had not focused on sensory integration but rather on teaching Nico fine and gross motor skills, was now back at the forefront. She would be in charge of implementing a sensory integration program to calm and reorganize Nico's sensory system. Our hope was that these efforts would lead to a more grounded Nico.

Among other tools, the occupational therapist suggested that we use deep pressure, either by giving Nico a massage or a deep squeeze. This same effect could be obtained by having Nico wear a weighted vest or covering him with a heavy blanket while sleeping, watching TV, or at break periods during therapy sessions. She also recommended rhythmic repetitive movements, such as swinging or jumping on a trampoline or an exercise ball.

So, we incorporated these suggestions during the therapy sessions and throughout the day.

And although the effects were not as calming as Adderall, we could see some improvement in attention in general and during the therapy sessions. The weighted vest seemed to be a winner—both while sitting down at the table during the therapy sessions and while doing tasks around the house. We had to monitor the use of the weighted vest though, as we didn't want Nico to become dependent on this tool.

Occasionally, we used the weighted blanket but Nico did not like it as much. We also bought a small trampoline at Walmart and it became a great way for Nico to spend some of his energy and practice his language skills (as he could request jumping on the trampoline during the therapy session breaks and at other moments during the day). At that time, we were working on expanding Nico's language by requiring him to use three- to five-word sentences (*je veux sauter sur la trampoline*—I want to jump on the trampoline). Nico continued to make slow but steady progress. As for my role as Autism Supermom and Expert on All Autism Topics, I just continued acquiring and refining my knowledge by going to conferences and workshops on different autism-related topics. The last two conferences had been particularly interesting and relevant as they were about homeschooling children with special needs, giving us examples of what and how to teach the French, math, and writing curriculums, among others. Around this time, I also went to a conference given by Dr. Steven Gutstein on a new method that was making the rounds in the autism community called Relationship Development Intervention (RDI). RDI is a family-intervention method that addresses the core symptoms of autism. It focuses on building social and emotional skills. More particularly, it teaches children and adults with autism how to learn communication and social skills and eventually develop relationships.

Developed by psychologist Steven Gutstein, it builds on the theory that "dynamic intelligence" is key to improving the quality of life for individuals with autism. Dr. Gutstein defines dynamic intelligence as the ability to think flexibly. This includes appreciating different perspectives, coping with change, and integrating sensory information from different sources (lights, sounds, etc.).[16] I began to look into this method with interest in the hopes of teaching Nico the building blocks of communication—necessary to expand his language.

During this last year, apart from being mom to Alex and Nico, I would be Nico's overall program manager, Nico's teacher, Nico's generalization therapist, Nico's speech and language pathologist, Nico's occupational therapist, Nico's RDI therapist . . . you catch the drift. There was no real time for me—Claudia Taboada. But again, I was so immersed, I was so focused on leaving no stone unturned in our journey to help Nico that I didn't even notice that *I had no identity* anymore. I was just going through the motions, measuring my self-worth and my self-esteem by how far I could make Nico progress. And since it was becoming apparent that Nico's autism was quite severe, every time he had a setback, both my self-worth and my self-esteem would take a hit.

I still remember a particularly difficult time during this period in which I was going through life like a zombie, physically and mentally exhausted but trying to act like a superwoman on the outside. Then came the "teaching of colors episode." The concept of colors was a hard one for Nico to grasp. We would later learn that for some autistic children, colors are very difficult to master, not because of lack of intellectual capabilities but because of brain and vision immaturity (for example, some autistic children cannot discriminate between different colors because they perceive them as sensory overloading and so overwhelming that they can hurt their eyes).

On that day, my objective was to teach Nico his colors come hell or high water. It had been almost two years since we had started the colors program and neither of the two ABA therapists had been successful.

I decided that enough was enough and that I was going to take matters into my own hands and teach colors myself. I used some of the props and materials we already had, like different color cue cards, cards of the same object in different colors, cards with only the name of the color in it, etc. I also prepared other academic material, like worksheets based on those I had seen in workbooks. I had a laminating machine at home and I had become quite an expert at preparing teaching material.

On that particular day, the objective was to teach Nico by using different methods—from matching pictures to painting and coloring, to playing with playdough of different colors, from drinking in cups of different colors, from matching colors to the written word. All were tried to no avail. Although Nico seemed to be having fun, I was becoming frustrated, desperate, and anxious. But I couldn't let it show. I couldn't let it show because it was a lesson and I was the teacher and I was supposed to have a neutral tone . . . but the more time passed, the more I realized I was becoming more and more despondent and it was just time to stop this—for Nico's sake and for my sanity.

After our session, I just let Nico be. We went to the yard and he jumped on the trampoline and played on the sandbox. I sat on the porch, had a glass of water, and just stared vaguely at the backyard. I was physically there but, mentally, I was gone. We stayed outside for about an hour and then we went to pick up Alex at daycare. And I was still on autopilot. Rob was on a business trip as he frequently was, so I prepared dinner for the three of us. I then did the night routine with both boys and went straight to work on the evening project, preparing teaching material for Brenda's session for the next morning. Once in bed, I couldn't fall asleep because of the anxiety and the fear stemming from the colors episode: Would Nico ever be able to learn something as basic as colors? Would Nico be accepted in the neighborhood school? Or any school, for that matter, if he didn't even know his colors?

The next day, after Nico's session with Brenda, we had an appointment with the occupational therapist and then with the behavioral psychologist, Dr. Roberts. As I was driving between appointments, I fell asleep at the wheel for a couple of seconds on a two-way road. Thankfully, on that day, the car didn't swerve and there were no cars coming at high speeds in the opposite lane, but we could have been killed.

I was physically, emotionally, and mentally exhausted. . . yet I kept going. At this point, I had lost touch with myself and no longer had the ability to reach within to ask myself the hard questions: Did I really want to continue being a full-time caregiver? Wouldn't I rather be killing it in my career and fulfilling my personal dreams and aspirations? Since I was so emotionally and mentally drained, I could no longer have these conversations with myself and have these moments of introspection. *I had no identity.* I was just living my life on autopilot from one stressful situation to the next. Why did I keep going then? It would have been so easy to just curl up under the covers and let Rob take care of things. Or even better just go inside the garage, turn the exhaust on, and let it be. What saved me were the little glimmers of hope that would pop up here and there along the journey. When I would begin to lose interest and motivation to go on, these moments of hope would give me the courage to stay the course. On that particular day, Dr. Roberts's session had gone very well, Nico had done a stellar job at the table session, and that lifted my spirits. I felt proud of Nico. I felt proud of myself. I felt proud of our teamwork. I would get a little dose of self-worth and validation that kept me going for that week. And that's how I continued to stay the course, to the detriment of my physical, emotional, and physical health.

That year was a roller coaster. In some areas of development, Nico seemed to be making progress; in others, he seemed to be stalling or even regressing. But we kept persevering.

TIPS:
- **Take care of yourself!**
- **I was stuck in this parenting whirlwind of responsibilities. Things were piling up. I had zero time to take care of my mental, emotional, and physical needs. And I *didn't even realize it*. I just couldn't get out of this labyrinth on my own volition.**
- **In hindsight, would I have done it differently? Yes. I would have made sure that right from the outset of my caregiving journey, I implemented self-care and stress resiliency tools so, no matter what was being thrown at me, I was not forgetting my own wellbeing in the process.**

Chapter 14: Perfect Programs

That year, we discovered two activities for Nico: the Bridge Reading program and the Swim and Gym Program for special needs. Both activities were held in the same area, about a forty-five-minute drive from where we lived at the time. Bridge Reading uses visuals and rhythm to teach children with special needs how to read.

I contacted the learning center's director to learn more about the method and see if it might be a good fit for Nico. I also wanted to make sure that we could get someone who would teach Nico in French. After the end of our conversation, I was sold on this reading method and asked the director to secure a spot for Nico. Three weeks later, Nico started Bridge Reading with Viviane. And this method/therapy would be a game-changer for him. It taught him to gradually appreciate the use of the written word, to learn the letters of the alphabet, to read words and short sentences, and to eventually learn how to read short books. Autistic people may not be able to speak in long sentences and hold conversations, but some of them, like Nico, are able to read. To build Nico's curiosity, Viviane would use big books that contained the words of well-known songs such as "Old McDonald Had a Farm" or "Twinkle Twinkle Little Star." She would slowly sing the songs and make sure that she would point under each letter with her index finger while singing. This would allow Nico to make a connection between the pleasurable activity of singing songs and reading words.

Viviane and Nico would also read together the books that were specific to the method. Nico loved these reading sessions, and after every productive hour of reading, Nico would always come out of Viviane's classroom with a big smile on his face. Viviane and Louise, the other wonderful teacher who replaced Viviane, would give us written feedback on the sessions and some homework to do with Nico during the week. And including this homework into our daily routine was truly a pleasure, as Nico would always be alert and happy while reading his words. As some of you may know, most autistic children are visual learners. In Nico's case, we realized that looking at letters and numbers was calming for him and made him more grounded. Eventually, when Nico began school, these Bridge Reading sessions focused more on the reading tasks he was doing at school.

So, while on Saturdays, we would bring Nico to Bridge Reading, on Sundays, we would bring Nico to the Swim and Gym Program for special needs. This program's main objective is to help children with special needs learn gross motor and fine motor skills as well as swimming. The educators (who were generally college or university students) work one-on-one with the children. The program is held at a beautiful complex with a huge gym and multiple pools where kids can swim. It was great to finally find an activity that was well organized and where the educators were caring and knowledgeable about autism. In that one-hour session, Nico would do some arts and crafts, play some games to work on his gross motor skills (like play ball toss, walk on a balance beam, play jumping games, etc.), and then he would have a twenty-minute swimming session.

For the first time in a very long while, I felt a sense of relief. We had finally found two activities where we could leave Nico for an hour without worrying about whether the people teaching him would know how to handle his autistic behaviors or know how to adapt their teaching to bring out the best in Nico.

The only drawback was that these activities were far from where we lived, and we would end up spending the weekend driving back and forth. This was becoming tiresome, especially for the kids. After about eight months, we decided to explore the possibility of moving to this area, as there seemed to be more services for children with special needs. One day, after Nico finished one of his Bridge Reading sessions, we drove around some of the nearby neighborhoods to see what type of houses were for sale. We began to do this regularly on weekends, even going to a few open houses, to figure out which neighborhoods we liked better.

As Nico was going to start school in September 2007, we had to start looking at schools around these areas as well. One day, by chance, we discovered one beautiful neighborhood with lots of greenery and a nice outdoor public swimming pool. And although this area was more English speaking than the one where we were living at the time, it had a French primary school (we were looking for a French primary school because even though Rob and I speak English, French, and Spanish, we were advised by a speech pathologist to only speak one language to Nico, and we chose French, Tom's first language). So, we set our sights on this neighborhood with the objective of moving prior to Nico starting public school. We called a real estate agent to begin the search for our dream house.

TIPS:
- **It is not easy to find extra-curricular activities geared toward children with special needs.**
- **Reach out to all types of special needs associations, special needs private and public schools, colleges who have special needs counseling courses, your municipality's recreation center, the local Special**

Olympics Association, and, other special needs parents to get tips on relevant activities for your child.

Chapter 15: Placement

It was now spring 2007. Nico had just turned six years old. Thanks to Bridge Reading and his own brain maturity, Nico was making slow but steady progress. In less than a year, Nico had mastered most of the ABA basic curriculum and had learned how to read short stories and do very basic math worksheets. His capacity for reading words, small sentences, and paragraphs had translated into progress in other spheres like understanding abstract concepts, such as emotions, that are very hard to teach to autistic people. Around this time, we also noticed that Nico had superior visual processing skills and was particularly adept at visual processing tasks such as detecting symmetry in patterns. He also was very good at building blocks and patterns following visual models. Despite all of this, Nico had a significant expressive and receptive language delay. Nico understood most simple commands and could request things that he wanted to eat, drink, or do, but he was not able to start or hold conversations. But Nico could understand the written word, which made it easier and more practical to explain things to him and avoid tantrums. Most importantly, reading brought Nico peace and joy.

As we were gearing to enroll Nico in the public school system, we contacted the local school board to begin the process. We needed to fill out an application and submit a file with a psychologist's report by the end of June. This report was necessary to evaluate Nico's cognitive capacity at the time. The file would be reviewed by the school board's academic advisor who would then invite us for an interview mid-August. A decision would then be made regarding which type of school Nico would be attending: a regular classroom in a regular school, an autism classroom in a regular school, or a special needs school. The type of classroom chosen by the school board would depend on several factors, including the severity of autism symptoms and intellectual capacity.

I contacted a private psychologist with an autism expertise whom I heard through word of mouth. She was available to do the testing within the next month and get the report ready by June. The testing was done at our home. She made sure that there wouldn't be any distractions in the form of sensory stimulation (no noises, no aggressive lighting, etc.). To our surprise, the test showed that Nico's intellectual disability had gone from severe to mild, especially when evaluating all the tasks that didn't require spoken language. But despite this cognitive progress, Nico still had a big expressive and receptive language delay. In addition, Nico still had a lot of autistic behaviors related to his sensory issues, specifically his hypersensitivity to sounds. The psychologist's report was ready on time and we submitted Nico's application to the public school board in June 2007.

At the same time, we were under contract on a house and the moving date had been set to September 15, 2007. So that summer was spent packing boxes and preparing for the move. Notwithstanding all the chaos, we kept up with Nico's home program. Because Nico would begin school full time in September, we would be phasing out Brenda's therapy in the mornings, and she was to finish her contract mid-August. We agreed, however, that during the summer, she would do some extra hours in the afternoon to allow me to prepare for the move. I would also sit down regularly with her to learn the programs she was doing with Nico. You see, with Brenda no longer in the picture, I would be Nico's sole therapist. But somehow, I was unfazed. I thought that with Nico going to school full time, I wouldn't have much to do on the cognitive or behavioral fronts.

TIPS:
- **A good way to gauge your special needs child's cognitive progress is to have them undergo regular psychological assessments.**
- **It is important to note, however, that IQ scores of children with autism may not be accurate reflections of their innate intellectual potential.[17]**
- **In the past, nonverbal children with autism were considered mentally retarded, and those who had difficulties in communication were considered intellectually slow. Now, it has become more widely recognized that autism has nothing to do with intelligence.[18]**
- **Even if a person with autism is unable to talk, this does not mean that they do not understand what's going on around them, including what is taught in the classroom. For an autistic individual to perform to the best of their ability on standard IQ tests such as the WISC-IV and the Stanford-Binet, they must be able to quickly respond to verbal questions and have well-developed motor skills. However, these are areas that are difficult for those with autism. Furthermore, autistic children, teens, and adults suffer from sensory processing challenges that have an impact on attention.**
- **These IQ tests may not tap the true cognitive ability of those on the autism spectrum and *modifications to the testing* may be needed in order to bring out the best in a particular child (like making sure the room is quiet with minimal sensory distractions, giving slow and concise commands, slowing down the pace of the testing, building a rapport with the child prior to testing etc.)**

The summer of 2007 flew by. Packing from morning to night was added to my list of things to do. Since Nico was at home full time, I would find creative ways to have him help me get rid of junk, clean up, pack, etc. As usual, Rob was traveling a lot, so during the week, I was often alone with the boys. Luckily, Alex continued to go to daycare during the summer, save for the last two weeks of summer, when we took a mini-vacation in and around Montréal.

An important piece of the move was preparing both kids, especially Nico, for what was going on in our house—having strange people come and see our house, the mess, the boxes, the packing—particularly the packing of his toys. To reduce Nico's anxiety, I prepared a social story explaining to him that we were moving to another house in another neighborhood, not an easy concept to explain to an autistic child, especially the fact that he was going to sleep in a new bedroom. I had been to the new house and had taken a few pictures of the inside and backyard and put them in the story. I read it to Nico every chance I got.

What had me more concerned was Nico's public school debut. We still had not heard from the school board regarding which school Nico was to attend. All we knew is that we had a meeting with the school board's placement coordinator in the middle of August. We really needed to think long and hard, and well in advance about how to approach the subject of school with Nico. This was going to be a radical change for him in that he was no longer going to be learning from me and Brenda in the comfort and tranquility of our home. Rather, he was going to be learning from a teacher in front of twenty children. We decided that another social story was necessary; this one focused on the new school.

While the craziness of the move was going on, I called for a brainstorming meeting with both Brenda and the speech pathologist—who was guiding me with the drafting of the social stories. I had multiple questions and concerns, including but not limited to: how and when to explain to Nico that Brenda would no longer be his teacher? How were we going to prepare Nico and ease his fears about being surrounded by twenty friends for seven hours a day? How were we going to explain to Nico the chaos at recess and during transitions (the noise, the kids moving in all directions, etc.)?

On August 15, we met with the school board's placement coordinator. Based on the psychologist's report of mild rather than severe intellectual disability, Nico was going to be placed in a regular classroom in a regular school with an aide. This was the school board's decision, and we agreed to it only after asking for the following safeguards: (1) that a full-time aide be assigned to Nico to help him adapt and model appropriate classroom behaviors. This aide should be knowledgeable about autism, sensory issues, and autism behaviors (2) that the teacher have all the necessary support from the school board with regards to understanding autism, adapting her classroom to reduce sensory stimulation, and modifying the regular curriculum to respond to Nico's particular needs (lack of attention, difficulty with writing and fine motor skills, very limited language skills).

So, Nico would begin his public school adventure in September 2017. Before I get into that, I want to explain my role of autism supermom, as well as some of the research about the effects that full-time or part-time caregiving of a child with a long-term condition can have on physical, mental, and emotional health.

PART 2: The Physical, Mental, and Emotional Effects of Caring for a Child with a Long-Term Condition Like Autism

Special needs parenting doesn't come with a manual. It comes with a parent who never gives up.

Chapter 16: Autism Super Mom

B efore we go on to the research and scientific literature confirming the plight of special needs parents, I want to give you a detailed overview of what my role of "Autism Super Mom" was at the time Nico was growing up. I'm still wearing multiple hats, but things are less intense now because I've learned how to prioritize taking care of my physical, mental, and emotional needs.

To be honest, I still look back and cannot believe how I did it all without having full-blown depression. This is one of the reasons why I wrote this book: I want to help you avoid some mistakes I made and give you a roadmap of how you can take care of yourselves right from the outset of your journey. But first, let's examine my multiple roles.

(1) Becoming an autism expert

As I explained before, when we talk about autism, we are talking about different spheres of development that are affected *at the same time,* including but not limited to language and communication skills, gross motor skills, play skills, behavior, attention, etc. These are skills that we take for granted in neurotypical children, but in children with autism they need to be *specifically* taught. This adds to the parent's feelings of stress and despair. And if there is one constant in autism therapy, it is that there are different schools of thought about which techniques are the most efficient and which therapies should come first, etc. Opinions change, new research is released. It is a never-ending task to stay abreast of the latest and greatest ways to help a child with autism.

As I have always been a lifelong learner, I didn't mind getting my hands dirty, so to speak. I decided to dive in and become an autism expert of sorts. First up autism in general and the ABA method of treatment. I studied, researched, read countless books, and attended conferences. I wanted to be competent when speaking with all the experts I met along the way.

When the world of sensory issues became apparent to me, I launched into that: workshops, books, appointments galore. I had to help Nico the best I could.

Next, I dug into communication skills as precursors to language. I had to find the perfect program for Nico. I learned all I could about RDI.

Next on my list: become an expert in addressing Nico's missing motor milestones. I studied kinesiology and movement therapies like Padovan (Neurofunctional Reorganization) and Braingym, among others. I also did research on play skills, diets, and the gut microbiome.

It was relentless. If credits were given for my work, I would probably have two or three PhDs in autism by now. At the time, I didn't mind. I was hungry for knowledge, control, and hope. I would finish every conference or workshop on a high, always trying to find ways to incorporate what I learned into our daily lives. And this was probably again to the detriment of my sanity.

TIPS:
- **Beware of the overwhelming amount of information out there on the internet and choose carefully.**

- **Stick to one or two complementary therapies and then when the milestones related to these therapies are achieved by your child (or when enough time has passed that it seems that particular therapy isn't a good fit), move on to another therapy that will work on another sphere of development.**

Nevertheless, I still believe that knowledge is the most important tool we can have as parents. Knowledge is power and it is important to invest in this knowledge so we can become successful advocates for our children before health care providers, specialists, schools, school boards, and even health and education ministries.

At the conferences, I would meet experts, but what I cherished the most was meeting like-minded parents who, just like me, were barely surviving but trying to do the best they could for their kiddos under the circumstances. Most of us were parents who once had careers, who once had lives outside of being autism moms and dads but who had given up our previous identities for our kids' sakes. And although we were physically and mentally exhausted, we were relentless in the pursuit of knowledge. We would compare notes and exchange phone numbers in the hopes that one day we would meet for coffee, but we were often too busy.

Aside from becoming an autism expert, I also became a warrior mom—one who would not let *anyone* mess with her autistic son's rights.

(2) Becoming the ultimate advocate

In those early years, I also took on the role of advocate. Because government funding was scarce or nonexistent (as it is today), I also had to fight for Nico's rights before the Ministry of Health and our local readaptation center. Nico was put on a two-year waiting list because he couldn't be diagnosed due to his age. This was unacceptable. I advocated for him and requested that we receive some direct public funding to implement our own early intervention program at home and that the government pays part of the therapists' salaries.

Because of my law background, I felt that I had a duty to fight for justice not only for Nico but also for other children who were in the same situation. That ordeal took about six months, and although it was stressful, it was satisfying to see some positive results at the end. Eventually, Nico, as well as other children who were in the same situation, would receive either some direct funding to pay a portion of the therapists' salaries or be invited to move up the waiting list and attend an early intervention program organized by their local readaptation centers.

This advocacy aspect of my autism mom role was satisfying to me on another level—it allowed me to flex my legal muscles. Having had to abandon my career as an attorney to care for Nico, it was refreshing to be able to use my abilities for a good cause. Advocacy became and continues to be a staple in my autism journey, and I continued to fight for children's rights before the school, school boards, Education Ministry, and other government agencies. Having decided to devote my life to my son's autism journey, I often felt that I had wasted seven years of university and another eight years of practicing law. This advocacy role gave me back some control, a feeling of self-worth and self-empowerment, as I was making a positive change in the world. I was not only helping my son but other kids in the same situation. To people's surprise, writing legal demand letters was actually calming and good therapy for me!

Advocating for my child is something that I continue to do until this day. And it is something that will become particularly important as Nicolas reaches twenty-one and public and private services for his population become nonexistent.

TIPS:

- **Try to find an activity or something that can give you back a feeling of self-worth, fulfillment, and empowerment.**
- **In my case, it was fighting for my child's rights, but it could be anything like participating in a special needs association or setting up a charity.**
- **The point is that your child's long-term condition should not be the only thing that defines you.**
- **Make an effort in all of this craziness to find something that makes you tick and feel like you are a contributing member of society.**

(3) Being Nico's de facto overall therapist

Becoming an expert and advocate was time-consuming, but the most exhausting role was that of overall therapist. As we saw in the previous chapters, my role as Nico's therapist gradually expanded to being an encompassing one. First, I was Nico's generalization therapist where I tried to use every second of his waking hours outside of therapy to make sure that he was applying what he had learned in therapy to other contexts. Then I added Dr. Roberts's therapy session and principles. Then, we added speech and occupational therapy to my already full load. And again, I was involved from A to Z in this new venture. Learning everything I could about these two therapies, being avidly coached by the specialists and incorporating the exercises into our daily routine. Then I added teaching Nico academics and Bridge Reading as well as working on communication objectives via the RDI method.

I was so determined to help my child that I left no stone unturned.

I would become any kind of therapist Nico needed and bring in others too. I would be a play specialist, a Floortime therapist, a Padovan therapist, a music therapist, etc. Regardless of all the work I was doing, I always felt that it wasn't enough. I always had the impression that I wasn't doing everything in my power to ensure that Nico was being stimulated in all spheres of his development. This race against time would become a constant source of anxiety and stress.

TIPS:
- **Don't be too hard on yourself.**
- **You don't need to leave no stone unturned. Stick to one or two therapies at a time and leave yourself and your child some breathing space.**
- **It is understandable to feel anxious and feel like you have to cover all the bases so your child will catch up to their neurotypical peers. *But they don't have to*! This is one of the biggest misconceptions out there with regards to autism. Your child has their own strengths and weaknesses and will develop according to their own timeline. Our autistic kids may reach their developmental milestones later or in a different sequence than their neurotypical peers.**
- **So don't feel beaten up if you forgot that speech pathologist appointment or if you didn't know anything about that new therapy that everyone is talking about or you are just too exhausted to do that ten-minute Brain Gym sequence with your child . . . Try to chill a bit (if you can).**

I was also mom to infant Alex, whom I also loved with all my heart. On top of everything. I had to take care of the house and drive to all the doctors' appointments, etc. It was never-ending . . . and *physically and mentally draining*. But, at the time, I didn't feel I had a choice. I just plowed ahead, trying to do everything in my power to not leave *any* stone unturned.

Now, let's look at the research and at the scientific literature.

Chapter 17: Chronic Stress, Physical and Mental Health Issues, and Premature Aging

The research unanimously shows caregivers of children with long-term conditions such as autism have a reduced quality of life.[19] Multiple studies confirm that compared to parents of typically developing children, caregivers of children with neurodevelopmental disabilities experience more mental health issues such as chronic stress, depression, anxiety, and burnout due to the ongoing nature of care.

In an article published in the *Journal of Autism Development Disorders* in 2013, B. Zablotsky et al. examined the association between child autism symptomology and the mother's quality of life and risk for depression. They concluded that the worse the symptoms and the greater the number of co-occurring disorders, the higher the risk of maternal depression and lower maternal quality of life. They ended their article by highlighting the importance of screening for depression, particularly in mothers of children with autism with behavioral challenges and comorbid conditions.[20]

Then in an article entitled "Stress and Parents of Children with Autism: A Review of Literature," Dr. Susan Bonis conducted an extensive review of research articles focusing on parental experiences of caring for children with autism. She used health research databases to understand more about the challenges these parents face and provide direction for research and intervention. She concluded that parents of autistic children score higher on levels of stress than other groups of parents and that "the daily challenges of caring for the child are endless and affect all aspects of the child's care as well as the parents' mental health and ability to manage the needs of the child and family."[21] Among the recommendations for research and practice, they included recommendation for parents to use meditation and mindfulness for stress management.

The research is also clear about the negative impact this highly stressful life situation has on the parents' health. According to some studies, chronic stress puts these parents at risk for medical issues such as high levels of the stress hormone cortisol and CRP, a biomarker linked to everything from colorectal cancer to diabetes to heart disease. In one specific study done by Dr. Nancy Miodrag et al. entitled "Chronic Stress and Health among Parents of Children with Intellectual and Developmental Disabilities," the authors confirm that special needs parents of this population of children (who eventually become adults with the same special needs) encounter severe chronic stressors, particularly those involving behavior problems and extreme caregiving need. The chronic stressors that these parents face regularly "can wear down the body, particularly the cardiovascular, immune and gastrointestinal systems."[22]

These family caregivers, especially mothers, are under an unimaginable amount of ongoing psychological stress. And it is no coincidence that when researchers go looking for a population that is likely to record chronic stress throughout most of their lives, they use the mothers of chronically ill children. In 2009, the Nobel Prize in Medicine went to Dr. Elizabeth Blackburn and her colleague Dr. Elissa Epel for providing genetic evidence that chronic emotional stress might shorten a woman's life. They discovered telomerase, an enzyme that repairs and lengthens damaged telomeres. Telomeres are the DNA-protein complexes at the end of chromosomes that control aging.

In their paper entitled "Accelerated Telomere Shortening in Response to Life Stress," Dr. Blackburn et al. studied mothers who were under chronic emotional stress because they were taking care of children with chronic diseases. They concluded that compared to the control mothers of healthy children, the mothers who spent years caring for ill children had shorter telomeres.[23] When telomeres become too short, cells can no longer multiply, and this can lead to premature aging and susceptibility to disease. Over the past decade, scientists have found links between shorter telomeres and risks for cardiovascular disease, diabetes, poor immune function, some cancers, pulmonary fibrosis, vascular dementia, osteoarthritis, and osteoporosis. In contrast, studies have shown that people with longer telomeres are likely to live longer and have a better quality of life. So, in essence, mothers of children who suffer from long-term conditions might have an increased likelihood of premature aging and of suffering from a multitude of diseases.

Another study published in 2009 in the *Journal of Autism and Developmental Disorders* established that some autism moms experience similar stresses to those experienced by soldiers in combat![24] In that study, Dr. Marsha Mailick Seltzer and other researchers from the University of Wisconsin-Madison followed ninety-six moms co-residing with their autistic adolescents and adults for eight consecutive days. They were interviewed at the end of each day and saliva samples were taken every four days to measure the moms' stress hormone levels.[25] In a companion study, the researchers followed up with the same group of autism moms daily to interview them about how they used their time, their level of fatigue, their leisure activities if any, and whether or not stressful events occurred. This information was then compared with data from a national sample of mothers whose children do not have disabilities. Researchers found the following:

- The levels of chronic stress experienced by the autism moms were similar to those of combat soldiers;

- The autism moms of children with high levels of behavior problems had the most pronounced physiological profile of chronic stress. The stress hormone levels found in these moms have been associated with chronic health problems and can affect glucose regulation, immune function, and mental activity.

- Autism moms reportedly spent significantly more time providing childcare and doing chores and less time on leisure activities than a comparative group of mothers of children without disabilities.

- The autism moms were interrupted at work an average of once every four days. For the other mothers, the frequency was fewer than one interruption every ten days.

- On a day-to-day basis, the autism moms were three times as likely to report a stressful event on any given day, were twice as likely to be tired, and generally had less time for themselves compared to the average mother of a typically developing child.[26]

Chapter 18: The Different Stressors That Affect Special Needs Parents' Mental Health

T he sources of stress for special needs parents are many. In the case of autism (and other intellectual disabilities), the following could be considered key stressors:

Challenging Behaviors

Some autistic people can display challenging behaviors. There are reasons for these behaviors which may include:
- medical or dental issues
- fatigue
- hunger
- thirst
- discomfort
- difficulty processing sensory information
- inability to pinpoint the source of pain
- over-sensitivity or under-sensitivity to sensory stimuli
- transitions between activities or places
- changes in routine
- inability to communicate what is wrong

The challenging behaviors that we can see in autism and some other intellectual disabilities:

- physical aggression like hitting, scratching, biting, hair pulling, etc.

- self-injurious behavior or self-harm like head-banging, hand or arm biting, hair pulling, face or head slapping, skin picking, scratching, or pinching, etc.

- tantrums

- repetitive behaviors

- pica (eating or mouthing non-edible items like dirt, stones, etc.).[27]

Stigma and Social Isolation

Research confirms that stigma—the negative social reactions and beliefs of others—increases stress for such autism parents. Children with autism are often labeled and stereotyped as weird, different, or odd, and parents are blamed for "bad parenting" and being "too lenient." I can tell you right now that there isn't a single autism parent who hasn't felt the glares or heard the ignorant comments of strangers in the grocery store cashier line blaming us for our kiddo's meltdowns or "bad" behaviors. As autism families, we are constantly worried about our child's behavior and what other people may think. This worry may translate into isolation. Indeed, some studies have shown that families may choose to isolate themselves to avoid uncomfortable situations at social events.

In a study published in the *Journal of Autism and Developmental Disorders*, Dr. Ruth L. Fischbach et al. interviewed 502 autism parents about their children's behavior and family experiences. They found a significant amount of isolation and even outright rejection of children with autism and their families.[28] Children were often left out of activities, some were teased or insulted, and others even physically bullied. This, coupled with most schools' inability to stop bullying, inevitably contributes to high parental stress. As for the family's exclusion and isolation, the child's rejection by peers is one factor, but the biggest factors are symptoms and disruptive behavior such as serious tantrums and meltdowns, aggression and threats toward others, and self-injurious behavior such as head-banging. The greater the number of these behaviors, the more isolated and excluded the family felt from friends and relatives. In fact, Dr. Fishbach's research found the following:

- Forty percent of the isolated parents said that they isolated themselves from friends and family because of their child's autistic behaviors.
- Thirty-two percent reported that other people excluded them from social events and activities.

Poor sleeping habits

Children and adolescents with autism suffer from sleep problems, particularly insomnia. Researchers estimate that between 40% and 80% of children with autism have difficulty sleeping.[29] The biggest sleep problems include:

- Difficulty falling asleep/insomnia
- Inconsistent sleep routines
- Restlessness or poor sleep quality
- Waking early and/or waking frequently

It is difficult to pinpoint exactly what causes these sleep difficulties in the autistic population. Some researchers have alluded to the autistic person's hypersensitivity to environmental stimuli like noise and light. What is certain is that this lack of sleep can have a negative impact on a person's life and overall health. Several studies have shown that in children with autism, lack of sleep can also bring about other problems such as aggression, irritability, hyperactivity, increased behavioral problems, and poor learning, affecting not only the child but everyone in the family.[30] One study showed that the parents of children with autism have worse sleep quality, and wake up earlier than parents of children without autism. Another study concluded that such sleep disorders in the child have a significant effect on parental stress.[31]

Financial burdens

Since parents have to reduce their workload in order to care for their child and therapies and other services are costly, another huge source of stress for special needs parents is financial strain. Lots of research indicates mothers of special needs children leave their careers in order to take care of their special needs child full time, which, in turn, reduces family income.[32] A recent study in the province of Québec estimates that half of mothers quit their jobs within the first two years following their child's autism diagnosis.[33]

Because of the lack of access to daycare, adequate rehabilitative services, quality education, and adult services leads, parents have to reduce their workload to care for their children. Indeed, according to one study, parents of children with autism may often have to work fewer hours than people whose children have other health problems or no medical problems at all.[34] This leads to an overall reduction in family income.

Additionally, all these services are expensive. According to Autism Speaks, autism care costs an estimated $60,000 USD a year through childhood with the bulk of the costs in therapies and special services as well as lost wages related to increased demands on one or both parents.[35] It is believed that these costs will only increase as children become adults and graduate from high school as education, employment opportunities, and housing are almost nonexistent. More specifically with respect to the employment of adults on the autism spectrum, more than half of young adults with autism remain unemployed and unenrolled in higher education in the two years after high school according to Autism Speaks. Nearly half of twenty-five-year-olds with autism have never held a paying job.[36] Studies have shown again and again that families may struggle to pay for therapies that are not covered by health insurance or provided by schools.[37]

Feelings of Loss and Grief

And, of course, there is the *emotional toll*. There is no question that when parents receive the autism diagnosis, feelings can range from relief (because they knew something was wrong with their child's development but could not pinpoint the problem and now they could) to extreme grief for the loss of the "ideal" child. In a study published in the *Research in Development Disability Journal,* researchers Manuel Fernadez-Alcantara et al. conducted semi-structured interviews of twenty parents and asked about different emotional aspects of parenting a child with autism. The authors concluded that "the core category that explained the feelings of these parents was unexpected child loss associated with shock, denial, fear, guilt, anger, and/or sadness."[38] And although these feelings may not be sources of chronic stress per se, they are always in the background and can negatively affect an already compromised mental state.

Chapter 19: My Thoughts

From my own experience, I can tell you that caring for a special needs child puts parents in a constant state of fight or flight mode and helplessness. I will also say that it is the moms who often abandon their career aspirations and dreams to become their child's primary caregivers; thus, they bear the brunt of this daily stress. Call it chronic stress, call it anxiety, call it despair, call it continuous mental and physical burnout . . . the struggle is real, and it is *unacceptable*. We are burning the candle at both ends. Not only are we full-time caregivers and sometimes our kids' therapists and teachers but we also have to manage meltdowns (that can happen at any time), we have to fight with school boards and teachers about our child's rights for a better or more adapted education, we have to manage all the therapies, drive to specialists and doctor appointments. . . . the list goes on. Not to mention that we do all this while being sleep deprived—as between 40-80% of our special needs kiddos have trouble sleeping!

But the thing is this: we are so used to this daily grind that we just accept it and go on as if this were the new normal. But it isn't. We are at risk of:

- having shorter telomeres and, consequently, having a shorter lifespan

- suffering from mental health conditions, such as anxiety and depression

- suffering from other diseases including, but not limited to, cardiovascular disease and cancer

- suffering from decreased immunity

- suffering from insomnia and fatigue

And this chronic stress doesn't end when our child reaches the age of five or even the age of eighteen. This stress can magnify when children reach adulthood as formal public schooling ends and there is a lack of adult resources across the board—from lack of educational initiatives to lack of employment services to reduced quality of health care and shortage of housing resources.

Caring for a child with a long-term condition is a lifetime contract. And I like to use the following metaphor that Dr. Roberts always used to remind us of: "caring for and parenting a special needs child is not a sprint; it's a marathon." It is the *marathon of life*. I didn't know then that I would become a marathon runner. Being one enables me to give you the most important takeaway from all this: *you have to pace yourself right from the outset* in order to avoid hitting the wall. In runners' language, hitting the wall refers to depleting your stored glycogen and the feelings of exhaustion and negativity that typically accompany it. This means that right from the start, we must take steps to preserve and enhance our physical, mental, and emotional wellbeing in order to survive and complete the race of our lives as successfully as possible.

I am here to tell you that it can be done, and my mission is to give you the tools to take matters into your own hands. You can and you will find the courage to make self-care a priority. Autistic children will become autistic adults. Children with other disabilities will become adults with disabilities too. It is imperative that from the very beginning of your journey, you understand the value of taking care of yourself so you can be the best parent you can be.

The main purpose of this book is to share with you my *transformational journey*. I've been there. I was once that mom on the verge of burnout, not one but many. I was once that mom who lost her identity in the whirlwind. I was once that mom who was living my life on autopilot just waiting for the next meltdown or the next fight with the school board to wake me up from my stupor. Don't get me wrong—I would not trade my Nico or my experience as an autism mom to Nico for the world. But *I did lose myself* . . . That is until one day, by accident, I discovered something that would give me my life back and save my sanity: a passion for running.

PART 3: Reclaiming My Identity and Prioritizing Self-Care

Chapter 20: School Begins

September 2007 came. The move to the new neighborhood was easier than I expected. Soon, both boys got acquainted with the new house and they seemed to love the huge basement where the playroom was now located. Since we had used a social story to explain the move to Nico, he seemed to be getting used to his new bedroom which I organized with a layout identical to the one at the old house.

Both Alex and Nico had their schools picked. Alex, who was now a curious and very smart four-and-a-half-year-old, was enrolled in a bilingual preschool fifteen minutes from our house. With curly hair and big brown eyes like his brother, Alex was now a perfectly bilingual English-French speaker and loved to draw. Nico was now six-and-a-half and would now be going to the neighborhood French public school. Since we had deferred school for one year, he would be starting Kindergarten.

I was all ready to have time for myself again. After all our hard work, Nico would be integrated into the public school system and it was finally *my time*. This was the opportunity I had been waiting for to get back to fulfilling my aspirations—personal and career-wise. *But no.*

School was a disaster. Nico had been placed in a regular classroom where neither the teacher nor Nico's aide was very knowledgeable about autism. We knew this knowledge was necessary to make it work for Nico and we had specifically requested this at our meeting with the school board placement coordinator before the year began.

The principal and school board were no help. Neither the teacher nor the aide knew how to handle Nico's overstimulation tantrums. Kids with autism can flourish and progress if the right supports are in place. But the school refused to provide that for Nico.

Seeing the lack of willingness of the school board and principal to accommodate Nico's autism, we decided that it would be best to have him go to this school just for a couple of hours in the morning, with me homeschooling him for the rest of the day. I would teach him all the academics that he could not get from school. I would also bring him to the myriad of appointments with specialists that we always had.

My life continued to revolve around Nico's autism: being his teacher, therapist, and advocate.

At the end of the 2007-2008 school year, the school board decided to place Nico in a special needs classroom in a regular school. We accepted this decision, hoping that things would get better. We believed that this setup could help Nico adapt and go to school on a full-time basis. Once again, we had high hopes as a family. *I had high hopes of returning to my former life and career.*

In September 2009, Nico began the second school. The ratio was smaller: eleven students to two adults (teacher and class educator). This, we hoped, would help Nico be less anxious and more open to learning. And I thought that I could finally start thinking about *taking time for me.*

Although this setup was way better than the last school, the adult to child ratio was still high in the class, considering that all kids were on the autism spectrum, had more behavior issues, and made much more noise. This would trigger a lot of anxiety in Nico, which could then turn into aggression (scratching his classmates for example). I started to get calls at different times of the day to come and pick Nico up because he was misbehaving. I kept asking the new principal to bring in a behavior expert or an occupational therapist to help Nico regulate and tolerate noise and other sensory stimulation—all to no avail.

Our initial discussions with the school board had been positive. We had been reassured that autism knowledge and expertise would not be a problem. We believed and looked forward to the school system to shower their expertise on Nico and help him grow and learn.

But this was not how it worked out. I continued to be immersed in autism land 24/7. On top of that, Rob was traveling for work regularly and Alex was going to a new daycare and needed to feel nurtured as well. But I just kept plowing away. *This had become my new normal. Overwhelmed* and *chronically stressed* were my middle name.

I didn't know better. It had been so long since I had had a conversation with myself—Claudia—that I didn't know if I wanted anything other than being Nico's caregiver.

Because at that point, Claudia had *lost* herself.

Here I was, a former labor and employment attorney who loved to go to court and dress up in business suits and high heels, now spending my days in sweatpants, barely having time to take a shower. I saw my peers getting promotions, being named partners at law firms, or becoming judges while all I could do was watch from afar. I was jealous, almost bitter. I felt that they were lucky not to have children with special needs, or not to have children period. The "Why me?" question would pop up in my head almost every day. I saw the possibilities of me returning to work as an attorney (even on a part-time basis) slowly but surely disappearing.

I was trying to stay positive and be this superhero autism mom on the outside, but on the inside, I was starting to crack once again. The always present chronic stress was getting worse and invading my mental space: I felt *helpless, defeated, hopeless.* This stress was wreaking havoc on my health as I was having difficulty concentrating, starting to get regular headaches, and becoming more and more irritable. I was also becoming despondent and had difficulty falling asleep. My mind was *always* racing.

Although I enjoyed being Nico's teacher and therapist, I was ready to hand it over to the school system and get my life back. But it was not to be. When Nico was younger, I would have periods when I would feel defeated and hopeless but, somehow, I always bounced back because I believed that once Nico would be in the school system, things would change, become less hectic, and I would finally get *my time.* But as time went on and the public school system's promise to accommodate Nico's needs did not materialize, I began to seriously doubt my capacity to get my life back *ever.*

The decision to stay at home to devote my life to Nico and help him overcome his challenges is a decision that I will never regret. What I didn't anticipate at the time were the complications that would arise from the lack of appropriate school resources and services. Having to deal with red tape and with school board administrators and principals who could not provide the accommodations Nico so badly needed was plain demoralizing.

The race against time was beginning to drag on *forever*. Not to mention this was beginning to take a heavy emotional toll on everyone, especially Nico.

I was sad for Nico. I was sad for my family. I was sad for myself. I was *burned out*—physically and mentally exhausted, emotionally drained, hopeless, resentful . . . *almost on the verge of a major depression—without even realizing it.*

Enter Sicas, my son's service dog . . . and *my life savior.*

So, my *transformational journey* began.

TIPS:
- **If you find yourself in a situation where you feel overwhelmed, hopeless, and physically and mentally exhausted *all the time*, tell someone (your partner, a family member, a friend).**
- **Difficulty concentrating and insomnia can also be symptoms of a bigger problem.**
- **Do not hesitate to consult a psychologist or another qualified professional.**
- **Your special needs child's social worker could also be a great sounding board and may be able to refer you to parents' support groups and other organizations that could provide caregiver support services.**

Chapter 21: Accidental Runner

"Out on the roads, there is fitness and self-discovery and the persons we were destined to be." – George Sheehan

In early 2008, we had heard that the MIRA Foundation (whose mandate is to train and provide guide dogs for the blind in the province of Québec) was conducting a study about the feasibility of providing guide dogs to autistic children. The premise of the study was that the dog would help reduce stress and anxiety in the family and improve the quality of sleep, language, and socialization of the child with autism. They were recruiting families for the study and, in exchange, the family would be gifted a guide dog. So, we applied, and in October of 2008, they told us we had been selected. We were ecstatic! We really didn't know if Nico would take to his dog but we were happy to try. So, in December of that year, I went to a week-long training at the MIRA Foundation headquarters in Saint-Madelaine on the outskirts of Montréal. I was paired with Sicas—the most calm and gentle black Lab.

Sicas came home with me four days before Christmas 2008 and it was definitely the best Christmas present for the family that year. Neither of the two kids was yet able to take her out by themselves and Rob would continue to travel often during this period, so I took on the added responsibility of taking Sicas out for walks. To be honest, I didn't like the added responsibility of having to go out regularly with Sicas. I was in over my head with parenting Nico and Alex and taking care of the house. At the time, I wondered how I was going to muster the energy to go out with the dog. Sometimes, I didn't even have time to take a shower, and now, I had to take care of this dog? I had more than enough on my plate!

As for Nico's academic learning at school, it was hampered by his distraction and his hypersensitivity to noise. So when I suggested to the teacher that I complement the learning at home (as it was quieter and Nico was used to working with me), she was all for it, even giving me suggestions and lending me some teaching material and lessons in French and in math. So, on the days I did not have to pick Nico up sooner because he was misbehaving, I still picked him up right after lunchtime to work the academics in a quieter environment with me. Our sessions would run for about four hours with a couple of breaks in between. This collaboration with Nico's teacher was one of the bright spots during this time. This kept me going.

At the time, my mornings consisted of doing some house chores, laundry and the like, and preparing material and lessons for Nico's afternoon homeschooling sessions. I was really not comfortable with taking time for myself and was literally scared to increase my stress level by "wasting all this time" with Sicas. But I had no choice. I wasn't going to let her poo on the carpet!

So, I reluctantly began to take Sicas out. I saw it as an extra chore. A necessary one but no more than an extra house chore. I would just go up and down my street because the sooner I could get back home to do my other activities the better. But a week or two later, something *magical* happened. I realized that I had started to *crave* these outings. Whereas before, I saw this as a burden, I was now seeing this as a good pretext to go out for some air. And who knows I may want to do like the other people with dogs in my neighborhood and do some fast walking or running! Heck, I had no choice but to take Sicas out, so I might as well make the most of it!

Yes, I was busy. But this was no reason to prevent me from taking time for myself. The reality was that things had been so complicated and crazy since Nico's diagnosis that I couldn't remember the last time I had gone for a leisurely walk by myself. *Things had to change.* And I decided that from then on, there would be *no excuses*! I was going to make the effort—snow, cold, rain, or shine—to get out there with Sicas and, in the process, get in some much-needed physical activity. I also decided that I would first increase the pace of my walks and then try running a little bit.

It hit me that it had been ages since I had bought myself a pair of running shoes. Were these people I saw outside with their dogs wearing some special winter running shoes? Did I need to get myself some special winter pants and a sporty coat? I was curious and actually getting quite giddy!

There was no question that this was new territory for me, or, at least, something I had not experienced in a long, long time— doing something for *me*. Before I had kids, my most athletic accomplishments were going to aerobic classes at the university, hiking, and a little bit of cross-country skiing. Apart from gym class, I did not do any sports like track or swimming in middle or high school. So Sicas was taking me out of my comfort zone and putting me on the spot. I needed to get outfitted to go for walks in the freezing cold, and I needed to do this ASAP!

I vividly remember going to the local running store and being all excited about the running clothes, shoes, and gear. I was a little self-conscious as I asked the girl at the counter (who was lean and mean and looked like a track star) about what running shoes she would recommend. Did I need some special shoes to run in the winter? Her response, "*We* runners just wear normal running shoes" (i.e., I was not part of the running gang. I was not a runner and didn't look like one at the time either). Looking back, I should have been offended by her answer, but I was not. I was just glad to be learning all these new things about this new activity that was taking me out of my comfort zone.

I followed the track star's advice and got some Asics running shoes. She also suggested that I get some winter running pants, some double layer socks, some wind-proof mittens and a winter running hat. All these were necessary to brave our crazy cold Canadian winter. As for the jacket, I remember having bought one years ago before I had kids. It was a cross-country skiing jacket but the woman at the counter assured me that it would be perfect for walking and running in the winter. So, the stage was set!

With this new mindset and some new running gear, I started taking Sicas out every day for walks around the neighborhood and just enjoyed the surroundings. Although walks were still not very long, I was no longer restricting myself to just walking up and down my street. I went along with Sicas to explore this relatively new city of ours. One day, we would go up and down Windermere Blvd., another day we would turn around and go on Sherbrooke Street. If we were more adventurous, we would go all the way to Elm Street.

Eventually, I realized that these walks were invigorating . . . and that I was slowly but surely becoming hooked! And at the time, I didn't know if this feeling was due to going outside in the freezing cold, the act of getting much-needed exercise, and/or being completely alone with my thoughts—I just felt *energized*. These walks felt liberating! Just getting out for some fresh air was something I had not done since Nico had been diagnosed with autism.

I was finally allowing myself to take some well-deserved time for me and not be chained to autismland anymore. And I started craving these walks with Sicas. Something that felt forced at the beginning became a habit and then a *necessity*. My body and mind were itching for their next adventure with Sicas! I started to like these walks so much that I gradually increased their time from ten minutes to twenty minutes. I know it's not much. But for someone who was still feeling guilty for taking time for herself, this was a huge milestone! That winter I learned how to brave the cold. Walking at -35C (-31 F) or in a blizzard was no longer an excuse.

By the end of spring 2009, I was ready to try running as I had been inspired by a very graceful runner who would run by my house regularly. She didn't run fast but she had a beautifully easy stride that I wanted to emulate. She also had a killer running wardrobe! I wanted to be like her one day.

So, in May I decided to finally try to run. At the time, I had no aerobic endurance and couldn't run for more than two minutes. So, I would walk for two minutes and run for two minutes. First, I started by going up and down the street, then around the block. I continued to walk/run like that three times a week until the summer arrived.

That summer, Nico was at home for most of the time, so I had to wait until Rob came home to go for my run. And it was *magical*. Every single time I would feel like a million bucks after my run! Always looking forward to the next run day. I was starting to fall in love with this *me* time.

In hindsight, if the absolute necessity and urgency to take Sicas out to relieve herself had not been present, I would have never allowed myself the right, or rather the gift, to take time for me. Guaranteed! At the time, I thought that my most important duty apart from being a mom to my two boys was to help Nico with his challenges. I didn't want to get distracted and dissipate my energy too much. Over the years, I've come to realize that taking care of one's self is key to being the best caregivers we can be.

TIPS:
- Taking time for one's self is not selfish.
- It's a *priority* and a *necessity* for everyone, especially for busy moms who are overloaded and overwhelmed: working moms, stay-at-home moms, special needs caregivers, etc.

Chapter 22: Permission to Take Time for Myself

"It all begins with you. If you do not care for yourself, you will not be strong enough to take care of anything in life." — Leon Brown

As I mentioned, one of my favorite analogies for parenting a child with special needs is that "it is not a sprint, but a marathon." This means that we, as primary caregivers of our children, need to pace ourselves accordingly *from the outset* if we want to be physically and mentally capable of handling the long-term whirlwind. This applies to all types of busy parents. Even though you may not have the same burdens as special needs parents, you still want to be present for your kids and be the best parents you can be. For this to happen, we all need to take the time *daily* to *nurture and take care of ourselves.*

Self-care is defined as "any activity that we do deliberately in order to take care of our mental, emotional, and physical health"[39] or the "practice of taking an active role in protecting one's own wellbeing and happiness, particularly in times of stress."[40] It's the *me* time that is so necessary when things around us are starting to get out of control. These quotes sum up my feelings about self-care.

- Heather Petherick: "Self-care is not selfish. It is the foundation for serving others."
- Eleonor Brown: "Self-care is not selfish. You cannot pour from an empty vessel."
- Katie Reid: "Self-care is giving the best of you instead of what is left of you."
- Mandy Hale: "It is not selfish to love yourself, take care of yourself and make happiness a priority. It is necessary."
- Unknown: "Self-care is not selfish or self-indulgent. We cannot nurture others from a dry well. We need to take care of our own needs first then we can give from our own surplus, a place of abundance."

We know that self-care is essential to our wellbeing. So, why do so many of us not take self-care seriously? Because we don't have time? No that's the easy answer. And I bet that if I were to ask most stressed-out moms and dads why they don't take time for themselves, 99% would give the same "I have no time" answer.

I suggest you change the way you look at self-care. Would you take insulin if you were a diabetic? Would you agree to have a blood transfusion if your life depended on it after a car accident? Well, friends, *I want you to view self-care as the internal faucet that gives you emotional anchoring in all facets of your life.*

As we will see in the next chapters, self-care can take different forms, but the unifying concept is the same: you have to make a *conscious effort* and give yourself *permission* to take time for yourself. It is the only way. No longer view "taking time for yourself" as a flexible commodity but rather as a *priority*.

TIPS:
- **Realize that physical, mental, and emotional self-care is not egotistical or narcissistic. No matter how busy you are, give yourself permission to take time for**

yourself. You deserve it. It's not selfish but *necessary*.

- **Start today:** *no excuses.*
- **Start small: ten to thirty minutes per day.**
- **Find something that brings you joy. Something where you can immerse yourself fully and forget about your daily routine.**
- **Get *creative* (paint, write) or get *active* like I did.**
- **Focus on yourself and forget the rest: Ideally no phones, no screens.**
- **You don't need to be an expert. You just have to enjoy what you are doing and, most importantly, lose yourself in the feel-good endorphins.**
- ***Just do it.***

Chapter 23: A New Setback

"Life is like riding a bicycle; to keep your balance, you must keep moving." —Albert Einstein

In the fall of 2009, Nico started his second year at the second public school. He was now a handsome eight-and-a-half-year-old with big brown eyes and the same mischievous grin he had when he was younger. He was tall for his age. Although Nico tolerated Sicas, he was not particularly prone to playing with her. However, he would eventually learn and enjoyed walking with her on a leash—it was calming and self-regulating for Nico.

On the academic front, Nico continued to make slow but steady progress, thanks to Bridge Reading and other academic activities I would do with him during our afternoon homeschooling sessions. Spontaneous language was still a work in progress and we continued to focus on the precursors to communication using the RDI method. Nico had started to make some strides in the public school setting the previous spring as he began to trust the teacher more and, therefore, began to feel more comfortable in class. We were hoping that things would only improve from there on during the 2009-2010 academic year.

However, we had some news that would disrupt Nico's school progression. Not long after the school year started, we were told that both the teacher and the class educator, whom Nico had gotten to know, like, and trust, were going on maternity leave. The new staff was chosen according to seniority as per the school board's collective agreement and it appeared that the need for autism expertise when selecting replacements was not a priority.

Again, we were faced with both a teacher and school educator who did not have much expertise or knowledge of autism and the behaviors associated with it. Because of this disruption, Nico started to act out of anger. He began to throw tantrums and not listen, sometimes being aggressive to the staff or even his classmates. *Once again*, I had to pick Nico up at all hours and continue to work with him at home. Similar routine as the prior two years with the added twist that sometimes I would get a call from the school's principal at 9:30 a.m. or right after snack to come and pick Nico up because he was being unruly and the staff could not control him.

This confirmed that there was a total lack of adequate public resources and services once a child with special needs reaches the age of five. The public-school boards do not have enough money nor the will to allocate resources to these classrooms. Teachers and educators are overwhelmed and unequipped to deal with children with autism or other conditions like ADHD, anxiety, etc.

This new setback made me realize once again that despite all the efforts and therapies to "save Nico from his autism," Nico's autistic behaviors were not improving. Nico was definitely more anxious from both the school's sensory overload and the change in staff. This anxiety was turning into aggression (scratching others) and tantrums. But the most worrisome part of it all was that this aggression was spilling into our home life. Nico, who had never been aggressive toward his brother or me, was now starting to be so at home. It was probably one of his worst periods in terms of behavior since the start of our autism journey. And it was very alarming.

Hope for the future was beginning to fade and I was again feeling *demoralized* and *hopeless*. One night, as I was picking up the dishes from the table after dinner, something set Nico off (I don't know if it was the sound of the dishes or some outside sound) and he suddenly reached out to Alex and scratched his face. This was the first time that anything like this had happened, and it was terrifying. I felt sad and mad at the same time. I had two babies I desperately wanted to protect. I felt inept and incompetent for provoking or being unable to prevent this aggression.

Poor Alex! Not only was he, as a sibling of a special needs kid, feeling neglected by his parents, who were busy taking care of his brother's needs, but now he also had to endure his brother's aggression. I asked Nico to apologize to Alex. I then put Nico in the corner and then sent him directly to his room. I cleaned up Alex's wound and put some antibiotic ointment on it and held him tight and explained to him why Nico was unusually anxious and why he may have reacted the way he did. I loved Alex with all my heart and felt powerless to protect him from the whirlwind. I was trying as best as I could to hold back my own tears. This particular day, Rob was stuck in a meeting at work. I had to keep it together for Alex and be strong for us all. After the kids went to bed, I waited for Rob to arrive. We hugged and I told him all that had transpired that evening. Our main concern being the emotional toll this was taking on Alex who had become a very curious, intelligent boy who loved his brother unconditionally. He had just begun first grade around this time. We were genuinely concerned for his mental wellbeing and hoping that this incident would not dim his joie de vivre.

As I finished the chores and was going to go to my room to cry my eyes out . . . I realized that I had to take Sicas out.

While I was still emotionally exhausted from what had just transpired, the thought of going out for a walk or quick run on a cold fall evening put a smile on my face. Yes, something was different from the previous years . . . I had this precious *time for myself* when I could just go, lose myself in my thoughts, or better, lose myself in the surroundings (when being alone with my own thoughts was too painful). *I now had an outlet.* I had this treasured *me* time that enabled me to deal with the ups and (mostly) downs of this period of our autism journey. I now had my walking and running to ground me and help me cope.

And no one could take this away from me! Because of all the sh** that was going on in autismland, I was more resolved than ever to maintain my running routine.

TIPS:
- **Special needs siblings are superheroes in my book. Not only do they get less quality time from their overwhelmed parents but sometimes, they must endure, cope with and witness behaviors like aggression, self-stimulatory behaviors (e.g., flapping, rocking), self-injurious behaviors (e.g., head-banging) and lack of emotional and social reciprocity.**
- **It is imperative that you explain to your neurotypical children the *whys* of these behaviors and give them concrete ideas on how to cope.**
- **If you notice that your neurotypical children are acting out because they may feel neglected or if they have distressing emotions such as guilt or anxiety, do not hesitate to consult a psychologist or another qualified professional.**

Chapter 24: Run the Risk—The Moment That Changed My Life Forever

"Life is all about taking risks. If you never take risks, then you'll never know what you are capable of." —Unknown

By the fall of 2009, I was running about fifteen—slow but continuous—minutes three times a week while the kids were at school. I had started to increase the length of my continuous running in the summer of 2009. That summer, I really started to enjoy running and pushing myself. It was not much, but enough to make me sweat: two-minute bursts of continuous running, then three minutes, four minutes, and so on. Sicas and I would go for a fifteen-minute walk first, then I would see if she was up for some running with me that day (unlike most dogs, Sicas didn't like running much!). If Sicas wasn't feeling it, I would just leave her by the porch on a leash while I did my "running thang."

First, I began by running up and down the street in front of my house, then I would go around the block, then up and down the whole boulevard, gradually adding a new street to my route.

That summer, I also discovered two things: (1) the Lululemon cute workout gear and (2) running magazines. As for number (1), I've always been a fashionista and loved colorful outfits. When I was an attorney, I loved dressing up in powerful suits and matching heels. I loved to use colorful scarves to add some glow to my work attire. But while immersed in autism land, I barely had time to get out of my sweat pants and comb my hair. As for matching outfits? Not even on my radar! So, when I had the opportunity to become a runner, I decided that I would look the part.

So, sometime during that period, I went to Lululemon for the first time and I fell in love. I absolutely had to get some cute tops, some tights, and running shorts. And let me tell you, just the act of taking the time for myself to go to the mall and look for some workout gear was such a powerful mindset shift! I went from feeling like a trapped animal and victim of the circumstances to deciding that I was going to give myself permission to think about *me*. I had not cared or thought about my personal appearance for a *very* long time.

This running thing was not only forcing me to take time for myself, but it was making me rediscover some facets of my identity that had been lying dormant for years since Nico was diagnosed. And yes, I realized that looking good while working out was good for both the mind and the soul! Cute workout gear and some lipstick and this gal was looking like a running babe, even though she could not run for more than a couple of miles continuously!

As for the running magazines, they opened my eyes to a new way of thinking about my body. Apart from an occasional browse at fitness magazines in line at the grocery store or at the local bookstore, I don't recall buying any fitness magazines since Nico was born. I had bought some fitness magazines pre-kids but they were more about the latest diet craze or how to get that booty ready for bikini season, but never in a million years would I have imagined buying a magazine about running! But that summer, I did. This was perhaps a sign that I was taking this hobby seriously. I discovered both *Runners World* and the now-defunct, but superb, *Running Times* magazine.

I still remember the first running magazine I ever bought: a *Runner's World* with two-time US Olympian Kara Goucher on the cover (she would become one of my running idols) and I was so curious that I read it cover to cover that same day! I particularly loved the articles in the *Running Times,* as they were more scientific and thorough and they would unleash the inner scientist in me! (prior to studying law, I obtained a degree in Biochemistry).

As I started to read these magazines, I realized that there was more to being a runner than having a cute workout wardrobe. I also needed to look at other aspects like nutrition, recovery, ancillary exercises to strengthen parts of the body other than just legs, etc. So, I decided that in addition to running, I would be adding a strength-training routine for my abs, arms, and back.

I wanted something that would be efficient and effective. I knew that Pilates was an excellent way to strengthen the core, so I decided to go for Pilates videos that I could do at home when the kids were at school or asleep. I made the time to go to the bookstore to look for some workout DVDs. As luck would have it, I found exactly what I was looking for: two Pilates workouts called *The 10 Minute Solution* with four ten-minute workouts targeting different parts of the body. I was sold! And as soon as the kids went back to school, I began my new routine: three or four times a week running continuously for fifteen minutes, short walks with Sicas during the day, and ten minutes of Pilates strengthening exercises (trying to do each body part once or twice per week).

This gal was on fire!

At the end of September, I went to a running store to look for some running capris, as the temperatures were starting to drop in Montréal. They had a table with some volunteers from the Breast Cancer Society and I stopped by to chat with the ladies. They were asking for donations and advertising a 5K race that happens the first week in October in several parts of Canada called "CIBC Run for the Cure." The race was on October 4—my birthday. And as I was about to give them a donation, something magical happened. I mustered the courage to sign up for that 5K race! I still can't explain it. There was some inexplicable force, something in my gut that told me that I needed to sign up for this race. I told myself that this would be a birthday *present*.

I realize now that signing up for that race was my way of telling my subconscious to keep going on this new path of self-discovery. It was a way to give myself a pat on the back for the way I had been keeping up with my exercise routine despite all the struggles on the home front. It was also a way to keep the curiosity and self-motivation going.

Obviously, the courage to sign up for this race could only happen because of the mindset shift that had begun to take place since I started walking with Sicas the previous winter. I was feeling stronger, both physically and mentally, and something like signing up for a race—which would have seemed ridiculous a year prior—was actually a scary but exciting challenge. Despite (or because of) all the struggles that were happening on the home front with Nico and his school, I decided to go for it. I also decided that as compensation for running this first race, I would give myself a present that would make my runs more enjoyable: getting an iPod and some more running gear, as winter was just around the corner.

I still remember that fateful Sunday, October 4, as if it were yesterday. It still gives me chills. Here I was, not having run more than 3.8K in my life and now attempting to run my first 5K race. How dare I do such a foolish thing? My biggest fear? To finish last. I was terrified at that thought as I didn't really know what to expect at a race. As I mentioned earlier, I was not very active growing up and never ran track in high school or university. I wasn't born with the "athletic gene." I had never run a race in my life. This would be my first experience lining up to cross a finish line.

I got up early to make sure that I would be at the race on time. Since I had no idea what to eat for race day, I just had my usual breakfast of oatmeal and coffee. The previous evening, I had prepared my playlist ensuring that Britney Spears's "All About the Music" would be playing a few times during the race. The race was to be at Parc Maisonneuve, a beautiful park near Montréal's Olympic Stadium. I got there an hour and a half early. Rob, the kids, and Sicas would join me later.

I was nervous, of course, still asking myself what on earth I was doing there. But my nerves soon dissipated. I started talking to the other runners and felt a sense of camaraderie right from the outset. It reassured me that some of the other participants were also racing for the first time, so I was not alone. The atmosphere was fantastic with loud music and volunteers, participants, and spectators all super enthusiastic.

It was early October but the temperature was a mild 17C. I was wearing long tights, a long-sleeve shirt, and a running jacket. As I began to line up at the starting line, I saw all these people racing in shorts and tank tops. I realized that I was way overdressed. But I did not have time to go drop off my jacket in the car. So, I just lined up with everyone else and quickly turned on my iPod to make sure that it was functioning properly. Then, the countdown began and the gun went off. It was go time!

I ran as best as I could. I thought that after 3.8K (my longest continuous run until that day), I would start to walk. But I didn't walk. To my surprise, I continued to run at the same pace. Somehow, I had the determination to keep going and push my limits until the end. And although I was there just to enjoy the experience, I still managed to sprint to the finish line! While running I was "in the zone" and I forgot my fear of finishing last. When I crossed that finish line and realized that I was not the last one, I was elated! And I will tell you *that finish line changed my life forever*. It was an epiphany. It awoke in me something that had been dormant all those years: it made me feel proud of myself, fearless, and empowered.

TIPS:

- **Take the risk. Do something that will challenge you and take you out of your comfort zone. If you never take risks, you will never grow.**
- **Look for something that sparks your curiosity, something that pushes your limits.**
- **If you are running, register for a race. If you are doing any type of creative activities like painting, buy yourself a bigger canvas, take a class, hold an exhibit.**
- **Give yourself little gifts along the way as rewards for sticking with the program. Get yourself some cool gear.**

Chapter 25: Taking My Physical Health Back

"Treat your body like a temple, not a woodshed. The mind and body work together. Your body needs to be a good support system for the mind and the spirit. If you take good care of it, your body can take you wherever you want to go, with the power and strength and energy and vitality you will need to get there." —Jim Rohn

After that 5K race, I was on cloud nine. We went for lunch to celebrate my birthday with Rob and the kids. I basked in the post-race glow for a few days and then resumed my walking, running, and Pilates routine. And I began plotting my next move. I had read in the local newspaper that a special needs association in my area was organizing its inaugural race to raise funds for their respite programs. It was the Oka race, which has since become a very popular fall race taking place the first weekend of November. At the time, they had 5K and 10K races and have since added a half-marathon. I registered for the 5K and continued to run as I had been, slowly adding some mileage here and there.

The situation at Nico's school remained unchanged. Because of the staff's lack of autism knowledge, Nico and the other kids in the class were getting anxious and more aggressive toward one another and the staff. I had written a letter to the principal to request that the teacher and the class educator be either replaced or be given some training on-site. We had even offered to pay for some training for the teacher and the aide with a behavioral psychologist or an occupational therapist. And if that couldn't be done, I told the principal that I could write a letter to the Ministry of Education to plead on the school's behalf for more financial resources to train the staff on autism. I received no response from the principal and was in the process of escalating the demand to the school board.

Throughout it all, I kept running. Before the Oka race, the furthest I had run was 6.5 km. On the day of the race, it was 12°C in the early morning, and this time, I made sure I dressed appropriately. The week prior, I went to the running store that was co-organizing the event and asked the manager how to dress for such conditions. On the day of the race, I arrived early to pick up my running bib and have time to mentally prepare. I noticed a table with a *switch distances* sign. I asked the volunteer what this meant and he told me that this was for people who were registered for the 5K and wanted to switch to the 10K or vice versa.

Something possessed me at that moment! I immediately had a vision of myself as a 10K finisher. I think that I must have had a smile and a twinkle in the eye because the volunteer asked me if I wanted to switch to the 10K. And without hesitation, I said yes! In hindsight, this was a pretty intrepid last-minute decision, as I had not trained for a 10K and I had never run 10K in my life! Yet, I was curious to test my limits and to see if I could pull it off because . . . why not? This running thing was making me mentally stronger and bolder. I ended up running the full 10K! Again, I was overjoyed and a bit bewildered by the fact that I was not the last one to finish. I felt empowered and ecstatic when I crossed that finish line!

This second race confirmed several things. That I had found my passion. That I was willing to do everything in my power to keep going, even when scheduling was hard. That the rush of adrenaline I got while standing at the starting line of a race was similar to the rush of adrenaline I would get as an attorney while waiting for the judge to arrive and hear our arguments in court. It was a rush that I had not experienced ever since I had to abandon my career. I had somehow forgotten this feeling and wanted to keep it alive. I was hooked!

After that 10K race, I had another realization. Because I had never been a particularly athletic person while growing up, I was in awe of what my body could do; being able to complete a 10K without stopping excited me, stirring curiosity over the possibilities for future athletic endeavors. I began to realize that my body was strong and that if I started to *take care of my health*, I could probably continue to push it. Without realizing it then, my new running hobby was teaching me more than just putting one foot in front of the other. It was making me aware that I was a person with basic physiological needs that had to be taken care of to properly function and even thrive.

These are the basic physiological needs that are at the bottom of American psychologist Abraham Maslow's hierarchy of needs. Maslow stated that people are motivated to achieve certain needs and that some needs take precedence over others.[41] Our most basic need is for physical survival, and this is the first thing that motivates our behavior. These basic physiological needs encompass, among others: nutrition, sleep, general health, etc. According to Maslow, if these needs are not satisfied, the human body cannot function properly. Once these basic needs are fulfilled, the next level is what motivates us and so on.

When a person is in a constant state of chronic stress (like a parent of a special needs child), these basic needs from Maslow's pyramid are compromised, therefore, making it harder for them to access the higher levels of the pyramid. We are *so* immersed in our day-to-day "special needs supermom or dad heroism" that we forget about ourselves and our most basic needs.

Discovering my passion for running and the realization that I could physically accomplish hard things led me to recognize that I *had a duty to protect this body* of mine that had me in awe. I needed to treat it with the kindness it deserved to become even stronger and more resilient. So, as my passion for running grew, I began to look more into my overall health, my nutrition, and the quality and quantity of my sleep. I concluded that I had neglected *all* of it. And I needed to do something about it . . . pronto!

First stop was illness prevention and taking care of my overall health. This was definitely a disaster area for me! I had completely neglected this aspect of my self-care. It had been ages since I had a routine medical exam, a mammogram, or a Pap test. Ages! Because I was accompanying Nico to all his medical appointments, I thought things were under control. I didn't even realize that these appointments were not for me! I was so not tuned to my body and to my health care needs at the time that a serious illness could have gone undetected in those years.

How could I neglect my health and my body this badly? Because back then the driving force behind *everything* I was doing was being a mom and helping Nico become the most independent autistic person he could be. Something happened to my mindset on those fateful two first races that empowered me and allowed me to look up and pay attention first to my physical well-being (and, as we will see in the next chapter, to my mental and emotional well-being). So that November, a week after my 10K race, I made a resolution to *take back my health*. I made appointments with a general practitioner, an optometrist, and a dentist for yearly checkups.

But that wasn't all. Because of those running magazines that I was buying, I began to look more seriously into my nutrition, hydration, and sleep. Although I tried to keep a relatively healthy diet for the family, my own diet left a lot to be desired.

Sometimes, I would skip breakfast and only eat at lunch time. When I was in a rush to appointments with Nico, I lived on coffee and nothing else or I would grab whatever junk was the easiest to grab, often not eating enough protein or vegetables during the day. I decided then that I would make myself eat three times a day and have a couple of healthy snacks mid-day. I would also try to have a balanced diet eating enough fruits, vegetables, protein, and some complex carbohydrates, especially now that I was being more active. I did not follow a specific diet. The objective was to not starve my body and to ingest the right amounts and a good variety of nutrients. This would alleviate any type of binging on junk food or eating the same lunch over and over (which I would do when I was particularly stressed out).

As for sleep, like many children with autism, Nico had troubles. Sleeping issues began when he was one. First, he had trouble falling asleep, then he would wake up frequently during the night or extremely early in the morning. We just accepted this fact as a family and did our best to cope. But I had never considered for a moment that sleep was so important to *my* overall wellbeing and recovery from workouts . . . until I began to read those running magazines. I had known for years that adults should sleep at least seven hours per day. But did I heed that advice? Nope! It really wasn't possible. What I could do though was to make sure that whatever sleep I was getting was good quality sleep. I also made a particular effort to go to bed earlier than before. So, I searched for articles on sleep on the web and began to explore ways to improve both the quality and the quantity of my own sleep (like doing a calming yoga routine or some meditation before going to bed) and that of the whole family.

As for hydration? I had no idea that it was so important for our well-being either. Again, I knew that an adult should drink about eight glasses of water daily, but I never did. It was not even on my radar! Sometimes, I would drink a cup of coffee in the morning, have a quick bite to eat at lunch time, and totally forget about drinking—water or anything else for the rest of the day!

So, I bought myself a big sports water bottle at Walmart. It was a twelve-ounce bottle that I would carry with me everywhere I went.

This running thing allowed me to turn around some very bad health habits that I had developed during the first years of our autism whirlwind. And you know what? I'm not ashamed of those bad habits and how I led my life during those early years. It was part of the journey and is part of being a chronically stressed-out autism mom. What I didn't have then were the self-care tools and the self-awareness that I have now, and for that, I'm grateful. And that is part of the reason I wrote this book. I want to make you aware, through my transformational journey, of the different facets of self-care that we often neglect but are so essential to our overall well-being.

TIPS:
- **Treat your body with the respect it deserves. Take care of it. Your body and your physical health are the foundation of the pyramid, and if the foundation is shaky, nothing can be stable.**

- **Make a list of the areas of your physical self-care you have been neglecting and then make the necessary appointments. Make slow but consistent changes to your habits**

  Illness prevention
  - **Keep up with your regular doctor, dentist, dermatologist, and optometrist appointments.**
  - **Get your breast exams, prostate exams, Pap test, etc. done regularly.**

  Nutrition
  - **Aim for balanced nutrition.**
  - **Don't skip meals; eat at regular hours.**

- If you are on the go, make sure that you have healthy snacks or healthy meals with you.
- Meal prep on the weekends if you can, so during the week, you can be efficient and just re-heat food.

Sleep

- Aim to get between six to eight hours of sleep per night.
- If your child has sleeping issues, try to go to bed at the same time as them.
- Avoid all exposure to screens (TV, iPad, cellphone) for an hour or two, but at least half an hour prior to bedtime.
- Establish a calming routine in the hour prior to bedtime: yoga, stretching, reading a book.

Hydration

- Aim to drink six to eight glasses of water every day.
- To remind yourself to drink regularly, buy yourself a bottle that you can carry with you everywhere.

Exercise

- Get regular exercise every day (aim for at least twenty minutes)
- Enroll in a dance class, a yoga class, a Pilates class, go for a swim or for a walk around the neighborhood, go for a jog or some cross-country skiing . . . the possibilities are endless. No excuses!

Chapter 26: Running to Calm

"Running is meditation on the move." —unknown

After I realized that I could run a 10K, I was ready for more! I knew then that if I didn't commit immediately and sign up for another race, I would not keep up with my exercise routine. And this time, I wanted to commit to a big enough goal to keep the hunger, motivation, and curiosity alive. I wanted a big enough excuse to stay consistent with my newfound passion. Once I realized that I was able to run 10K, the possibilities were wide open. After looking around for any interesting spring races, I decided to sign up for the Ottawa Half-Marathon the following May. I also decided to run a 10K race in the lead up to Ottawa as a tune-up race.

The situation with Nico's school at the time was very tense. It was November already, and it was clear that the new teacher and the new class educator were not able to help Nico. From all my research, I knew that if you're unsure how to prevent and deal with the challenging behaviors, you are bound to make them worse. That was exactly what was happening in Nico's class. Several of the children, including Nico, were becoming extremely anxious and generally more disorganized. Around December, we again offered to pay for an occupational therapist to come and observe Nico and give some suggestions to the teacher and class educator about strategies to help Nico focus and tolerate the noise and other sensory stimulation.

We considered pulling Nico from the school, but for the sake of routine, we kept him there but only in the mornings and not for lunch as the lunch hour was particularly noisy and chaotic. So, I continued to pick Nico up from school, but now even earlier than before. Sometimes, we would do some reading, cook together, and then have lunch. After lunch, Nico would have a TV break and then we'd get back to work.

Nico enjoyed cooking, and it's still an activity that we do regularly. On those days that Nico was home early from school, we would pick a recipe together and assemble all the ingredients at the kitchen table. We also had our own utensils and kitchenware. I had the big bowls, the big measuring cups and spoons, and Nico had his own plastic bowl, plastic measuring cups, and utensils. Nico's favorite cooking activity was to make chocolate muffins, so I began to adapt and vary the recipe to include grated zucchini, grated carrots, mashed bananas, apple slices, etc.

"*Je casse les oeufs*," ("I crack the eggs") I would say animated. I would take one egg, pause, look expectantly at Nico and wait for him to look. Once I had his gaze, we would nod together and then attempt to crack the egg at the same time.

"*Je verse le lait!*" ("I pour the milk"). I would then grab my measuring cup with milk, look at Nico with a big smile on my face, and wait for him to take his plastic measuring cup. Sometimes, if he wasn't paying attention, I would just make some funny noises with my mouth and pretend that I was pouring the milk and then he would look and join in the fun.

And I would follow the same pattern for incorporating the melted butter and the fruits and vegetables to the mix.

But Nico particularly loved mixing all the ingredients. I would wait expectantly and then go: "*Je mélange vite, vite, vite*" ("I mix fast, fast, fast") and then I would take my spoon, wait for Nico to take his spoon, and we would both mix with vigor. Suddenly, I would stop. "*Je mélange l-e-n-t-e-m-e-n-t*" ("I mix s-l-o-w-l-y") and then wait for him to join me in mixing very, very, slowly, exaggerating my movements. And so on.

Although I was using the RDI method to work on language precursors like nonverbal communication and imitation, this did not seem like work because we were having so much fun, and it was a great bonding activity for both of us!

During this time, Nico continued to make steady progress with his reading skills. He was beginning to read longer texts and do easy worksheets to work on his reading comprehension. So, I made sure that he completed his Bridge Reading homework every single day and that we read a few stories during our homeschooling sessions. It was so gratifying to see him focus and enjoy reading words and sentences! When Nico read sentences, he would sometimes look at me with a smile to share his enjoyment. I would always tell him how proud I was of him and how happy he made me feel, but because of his language and communication challenges, I would never get a response. But I *knew* deep inside that Nico was proud of himself and happy for making me proud. When Nico did activities that were mentally challenging but within his comfort zone (and within his sensory comfort level), all his autism mannerisms and behaviors seemed to disappear. He seemed content and at peace.

During our homeschooling hours, we also incorporated periods when Nico was learning how to do independent tasks himself, like making his bed, doing laundry, emptying the dishwasher. These tasks needed to be taught visually in a very detailed and sequential manner and repeated daily to become ingrained. So, I prepared visual schedules for all types of activities, from brushing teeth to making toast to giving Sicas her meal.

Around this time, my mornings consisted of (1) preparing my lessons and all materials to teach Nico in the afternoon (2) getting my exercise in—because even though I had less time for me, *exercise was already becoming a part of my daily routine*. I had upped my daily exercise fix from twenty to about forty-five minutes during weekdays and another forty-five minutes either Saturday or Sunday. I would run every two days. On the days I didn't run, I would do the ten-minute Pilates tapes.

Because I had to pick Nico up earlier from school, I had to be super efficient with my time in the mornings. So, after both kids were off to school, I would immediately get my run or Pilates in. To save time, I finished my exercise, prepared my breakfast (which at the time consisted of oatmeal, a piece of fruit, and a cup of coffee), and went directly to my home office to prepare whatever lessons or materials were needed for Nico's afternoon sessions. I would wait until Nico was having his TV break to take a quick shower.

No matter how hectic life was, there was no turning back to my old ways. Exercise was part of my life now and there was absolutely no way that I was going to stop this new journey of transformation. *No way*!

I had found the perfect self-care tool for me. Aside from the fitness aspect, the reason I stuck with running as my go-to self-care tool was the way it was helping me cope with the ever-present chronic stress. Indeed, studies have shown that virtually any form of physical activity can act as a stress reliever.[42] Physical activity can pump up our feel-good endorphins and other natural neurochemicals that enhance our general sense of well-being.[43] No other previous hobby of mine, including, gardening, or painting, had worked its magic quite like running had.

During the early years of my autism journey, I discovered gardening and dabbled in some occasional oil painting. And although both hobbies were able to take my mind off autism, they were not as encompassing as running was. For one, gardening was only seasonal. I loved painting and I actually discovered early on that I had a talent for oil painting, but for me, it was a complicated hobby to adopt daily. I needed at least three hours of uninterrupted time to set up my materials, mix my colors, and actually paint. With all the stuff going on at home, it was difficult for me to take all this time to set up and relax while painting.

I quickly realized that nothing beats the simplicity of running—I just grabbed my running shoes and went outside! In addition, the feel-good endorphins that came with getting some fresh air and moving my body was, and continues to be, second to none for me. There was no question that every time I laced up and went for my run, I felt *alive* every single time! And I can tell you that what runners call "Runner's High" is real. "Runner's high is a feeling of euphoria coupled with reduced anxiety and a lessened ability to feel pain."[44] It is said that "experiencing a runner's high is one of the best ways to feel happy and relaxed"[45] and I believe it.

Multiple studies have also stated that regular aerobic exercise provides several mental health benefits. For instance, some research has concluded that jogging or brisk walking reduces the symptoms of clinical depression.[46] The Anxiety and Depression Association of America compiled studies stating that running and other vigorous forms of exercise can reduce anxiety symptoms and help you relax.[47] In essence, running helps not only with stress management but also boosts the body's ability to deal with mental tension and anxiety.

TIPS:
- **Realize that you have the power not to let stress overpower you or control you.**

- Make a list of the three biggest stressors in your life and find activities you can incorporate daily to relieve that stress.
- You want activities that will make you happy, give you energy, and give you the belief that you can handle anything that life throws at you. **Walking and running are two of the greatest stress relievers out there. Give them a try!**

Chapter 27: Running for My Mind

"Running is cheaper than therapy." —unknown

So, I began to train for my first half-marathon in January of 2010. At the time, I was not following any specific training plan. Registering for races was my way of staying accountable to myself and to keep the motivation going. *Running was and still is my sanctuary*—and it was something that I could control. I ran from the pain, from the chronic stress of caring for Nico, and from the fear and anxiety for Nico's future.

At that time, I still had no coach. My coach was my mind and my own willingness to keep running consistently between forty-five minutes to an hour every two days—always making sure that I ran easy most days. And let me tell you that this gal was feeling damn proud of herself for finally taking exercise seriously since Nico's diagnosis. This "running thing" was slowly but surely becoming a *passion*.

And it had become a *necessity for my mental and emotional health*. Running was making me not only physically strong but also mentally stronger. Every time I ran and raced, I felt empowered. A feeling that I had rarely felt ever since Nico had been diagnosed. Running had become my *mental health fix*. It was the *me* time that enabled me to cope with the ups and downs of parenting Nico. And I came to enjoy, almost crave, the moments of introspection that this new running hobby provided me. Running gave me the opportunity to be with myself to look more closely into my situation.

For the longest time, I had been driven by the belief that I could do it all. I wanted to learn as much as I could to help Nico. I was going to be the Super Autism Mom who was not only the mom but also the therapist, the speech pathologist, the occupational therapist, the case manager, the advocate, etc. I was the invincible woman who had the power to shoulder all the responsibility for Nico's condition. In reality, the supermom was barely surviving—physically and mentally. *I needed an outlet, something that would help me cope with the never-ending stress.* And that's how running became my sanctuary and . . . *my therapy.*

I trained for the Ottawa Half-Marathon in earnest. Rain, shine, or snow, I kept running. In the spring of 2010, I began to increase the length of my runs. Usually my weekly runs were about 5-8K. My longest run to date had been the 10K race I had done the previous November. And I was quite happy to stay in my comfort zone. But since I had signed up for a half-marathon at the end of May 2010, I needed to start ramping up the mileage. So, I began to add a street here and a street there. Then another run or two around the block until one day in early April, I ran 13K mid-week! 13K was by far the farthest I had run in my life!

And while I was basking in the glow of my longest run and about to prepare myself a smoothie, I received a call from the principal's office to come and pick up Nico *immediately.* They had actually tried to get in touch with me earlier, but I had left my phone at home while I went for my run. They tried to contact Rob, but he was in a meeting. Apparently, Nico was not having a good day, was restless, and was more anxious than usual. He was scratching whomever came into contact with him that day—staff and classmates. I left immediately. I didn't have time to change or finish making my smoothie . . . I just went straight to the school to pick up Nico. By the time I arrived, Nico was exhausted and sleeping at his desk. Of course, I felt guilty for not picking him up earlier.

For a flicker of a second, I felt selfish to have been on my run while all of this was going on. But then my mind switched back and focused on the realization that it was up to the school and the teacher to handle Nico's behavior and make sure that he was not a danger to himself or others. After all, this was a specialized class where both the teacher and the aide were supposed to be "specialized in autism." It turns out that apart from some piecemeal training they had in autism, nothing else was being done either by the principal or the school board with regards to the level of training I had requested in my letters.

These poor kids were not being cared for as they should and because of that, they could develop even worse behaviors than those they started with. I made it my mission to try to improve the conditions of the children in Nico's class. On that day, however, the only thing that I could do was to take Nico home and try to reduce his anxiety as much as I could, even if this meant keeping him at home for a full two weeks, which is what we did.

On those weeks that Nico stayed at home, I homeschooled him all day. But because of my new found passion for running, I made sure that I could get my run in somehow, even if it meant running very late at night or very early in the morning. *Knowing that I had my release every day was reassuring to me.* Even if I was teaching Nico morning and afternoon, I knew that my mental health break was just around the corner.

I gradually increased the length of my Saturday runs until one day I reached 18K! That was three weeks before the Ottawa Half-Marathon. As the race approached, we decided to make race marathon weekend a family affair. So, we would go as a family and try to enjoy the weekend as best as we could. Unfortunately, because of Nico's hypersensitivity to sounds, he had a very hard time with the crowds. Although we managed that weekend, it was a bit distracting to me as I needed to be "in the zone" to mentally prepare for my race.

I had no other objective but to finish the marathon happy and without injuries. Mission accomplished! And with a very respectable time of two hours four minutes. I wanted more!

TIPS:
- **Anxiety, depression, brain fog, and other types of mental health issues may be part of your special needs caregiving journey.**
- **Don't wait to make your mental health a priority.**
- **Make a conscious effort to incorporate *mental self-care moments* into your daily routine. It could be as easy as some deep breathing exercises, a ten-minute meditation break, a fifteen-minute walk around the neighborhood, or taking a quick Epsom salt bath before everyone wakes up.**

Chapter 28: Being Flexibly Consistent

"Keep showing up." —Desiree Linden

E mpowered by my half-marathon endeavors in Ottawa, I decided to register for the Toronto Waterfront Half-Marathon, which would take place mid-October 2010. Toronto has always had a special place in my heart because I completed one year of practice there prior to passing the bar exams and officially becoming an attorney. In addition, my bestie from my law school years, Gina, lives there. It was going to be a great excuse to come and see her.

On the autism front, there was an impasse with the school and the school board. Neither the school nor the school board was willing to invest any money in training for the staff, and we were no longer willing to put Nico through the hell he was going through at school. We needed a solution. Two weeks before the end of the school year, we had a meeting with the school principal, a representative from the school board, and our social worker. The school board had a solution: yet another school! One where kids with more severe cases of autism went, one that was supposed to have the best autism resources in the province or at least our area. At first, we were hesitant because of the danger of Nico picking up more maladaptive behaviors from his classmates. But we decided to try it after the great sales pitch from the school board rep. So, in September 2010, Nico went to yet another public school.

That summer, Nico went back to the Adapted Swim and Gym Summer Camp for five weeks. Because of Nico's behaviors and sensory issues, regular summer camps were out of the question. During those two hours of Nico's camp each day, I would either go for a run or spend my time reading autism books. Thankfully, I was able to find Alex a summer camp with tons of fun activities near our house.

When I didn't run in the morning, I would go in the evening while Rob looked after the kids. When Rob was out of town, I would wait to see if Nico would take a nap and go for a quick twenty minutes run around the block. If Nico wasn't up for a nap, I would bring him with me to the municipal outdoor pool where I would ask a lifeguard to keep an eye on him while he played in the shallow end of the pool. I would then take the opportunity to run between ten to twenty minutes around the park beside the pool.

The lengths of my weekly runs between this period ranged between ten minutes to forty-five minutes, but I continued my attempt to run at least four times a week. Weekend long runs were complicated as we had lots of activities with the kids that summer, so I would just run on Saturdays or Sundays when there was a chance I would run a race on the weekend.

That month, I had another epiphany: I realized that I had physical endurance and that I was not afraid of running long distances. Within a ten-day span, I ran the Sainte Anne de Bellevue 20K race on a Sunday, the Mont-Tremblant Half-Marathon the following Saturday and the Dollard Désormeaux 5K race on the following Wednesday. I still had no coach and wasn't aiming for a specific time, but I had some decent finishing times all considered.

School for the boys would begin in a couple of weeks, so we were busy with back to school shopping, uniforms, and the like. We hoped for Nico, that this school would be *the one*. And we sincerely believed that: (1) there would be no more switching of schools, as this was causing the family and, especially, Nico anxiety and huge stress, and (2) dust would finally begin to settle in our ongoing battle with the school board.

Both these issues had been so mentally draining (especially for me, as I was the one fighting the battles) that we considered pulling Nico out of school altogether. But we decided to give the school system one last chance. The school board representative had been very persuasive at the last meeting, and we owed it to give Nico the chance to try this new school. We also wanted Nico to have a routine outside of the house: take the school bus, see other adults, interact with his peers, do different activities, and, most importantly, learn new things and develop his full potential.

TIPS:

- To stay *consistent* with your self-care moments, you need to be *flexible*. Flexibility is particularly important for busy people like us. *Keep showing up.* If you have to switch from morning to evening or temporally reduce the time you commit, do it, but please *stay consistent*. Identify what is keeping you from staying consistent (at least four days a week) with whatever your thing is.
- Make a list of the three optimal times in your day or week when you won't be interrupted.
- Make a list of those people who can help you stay consistent by taking care of your kids.
- If you don't have a village, then hire help if you can.
- Add your self-care moments to your calendar and plan your days to ensure that these activities are locked into your weekly schedule.
- Announce plans to others to increase commitment and accountability.

Chapter 29: Learning to Live in the Moment

"Living in the moment means letting go of the past and not waiting for the future. It means living your life consciously, aware that each moment you breathe is a gift." —Oprah Winfrey

Once the kids started school, I began to train for the Toronto Half-Marathon to the best of my abilities. I tried my best to follow a training plan outlined in an article in the *Running Times* magazine. And although scheduling the long runs was complicated, I still managed to run a 14K, 16K, and 18K in the lead up to the race. Because of Nico's difficulty with crowds and noise, Rob and I decided that it would be best for me to go to Toronto by myself. I also wanted to take advantage of this time to see my friend Gina, whom I had not seen for nearly ten years.

Apart from getting to run in a city I had fallen in love years prior, this solo trip would turn out to be one of the greatest discoveries in my journey to reclaiming my identity. From the minute I arrived in Toronto to the minute I left, I did not think about autism *once*. Of course, I called Rob and the kids a couple of times that weekend to see how they were doing and tell them about my race, but not once did I think about my fights with the school board, Nico's therapies, behaviors, academics, future, the impact of Nico's diagnosis on Alex, etc.

In Toronto, I had time to enjoy the expo. I was mesmerized by the energy, the gear available, the conferences, and the great quality speakers. I was like a kid in a candy store, loving every second of it! This was all about my passion, and all the people around me were as crazy about running as I was. That evening, my friend Gina and I went for an early Italian dinner to catch up and we had an absolute blast reminiscing about the old days.

On race day, I woke up at four in the morning to have an early breakfast, get ready, and prepare my nutrition for the race. I still remember getting in the elevator around dawn when in came young women of about eighteen, all dressed up and half-drunk. They were all staring at me—looking perky and healthy in my matching running outfit, my pony tail under my cap, and my lipstick matching my nails. One of them blurted "OMF***ing God. You look amazing; I want to be like you one day." I smiled back and said, "You just made my day, girl."

Here I was, being complimented for my athletic look, I guess. And, of course, deep inside I felt like an imposter—someone who just two years prior was so immersed in the chronic stress of daily caregiving that she had forgotten she existed. And at that moment, *I felt alive*. I felt like a million bucks! I was empowered and that little exchange in the elevator was the boost I needed to have a great race.

The weather was coldish and I loved the flat course. I crossed that finish line under two hours and beat my personal best by six minutes. I was over the moon. After I got my medal and ate a snack, I went back to the site where the medal ceremony was taking place. Saw the winners receive their medals and my eyes filled with tears of joy. I was happy to see these winners with their medals, I was happy to see all these crazy runners exhausted but so damn proud of themselves, I was happy to be here and take a break from the daily grind. I wanted to capture this magical moment forever and bring it with me so that I could recall it any time I felt discouraged in my journey.

I came through the revolving door of my hotel and on the comfiest sofa in the lobby were two runners. Bibs still pinned to their chests, they seemed to be falling asleep. The medals they wore were different than mine—they were marathon medals. "Next year, I coming back for *that* medal," I told myself in no uncertain terms.

I returned to Montréal, re-energized, and with a full heart. This was the first time since Nico had been diagnosed that I had been alone with my thoughts for longer than my runs or my races had allowed me. This solo trip would be another epiphany in my transformational journey.

And Rob and I agreed that from that moment on, I would schedule at least two solo race weekends per year, as these short trips were the perfect way for me to take a break from my Super Autism Mom role and an excellent way to recharge my batteries. These solo weekends also allowed me to get back in touch with friends. They became a necessity in my self-preservation toolbox. Why? Because during these solo trips, I was *in the present moment*. I didn't think about autism, or the past, or the future; instead, I thought about things like my gear and my running outfit, my nutrition, my race strategy, etc. Eventually, these experiences taught me that "being in the moment" (or what we call *mindfulness*) is crucial when managing the chronic stress associated with the caregiving of a child with special needs. In my next book, *Rediscover the Unstoppable Badass in You: The Busy Women's Guide to Self-Care, Fitness, Stress Management and Living Your Best Life,* I will expand more about mindfulness and techniques to help with stress reduction.

Fear for a child's future is probably one of the heaviest burdens to carry. This is on top of the pervasive emotional suffering and chronic stress that is a constant in our everyday lives. For the longest time, my fear for Nico's uncertain future invaded my mental space to the point of being paralyzing. Every single day, I had visions of Nico being left alone in this world once Rob and I are gone. Or worse, I would think about my poor Alex not fulfilling his own dreams and family life because of the burden of caring for his autistic brother. And if I wasn't thinking about the future, I would be thinking about the past—full of regrets about missteps along the way. In short, I was either thinking about the future or the past, but this was definitely not a healthy mental space to be in. I realized that by thinking about the future or the past, I was robbing myself of the little joys of everyday life.

Only when I started running and doing these solo trips did I get back in touch with myself and learned to live *in the present moment*. With running, I was tuned to my stride, my pace, the surroundings, my feet on the ground, my heart rate. On my solo race trips, I tuned into getting to the hotel from the airport, getting my race bib on time, going to the grocery store, and getting my race fuel.

Anything to make me *appreciate the present moment*.

I will expand more about mindfulness in my next book. For now, let me review some key elements. Mindfulness is a mental state achieved by focusing on one's awareness of the present moment, while calmly acknowledging and accepting one's feelings, thoughts, and bodily sensations, used as a therapeutic technique.[48] Mindfulness involves acceptance, meaning that we pay attention to our thoughts and feelings without judging them.[49] Mindfulness has been found by scientific research to be a key element in stress reduction and overall happiness. Being mindful makes you savor the pleasures of life as they occur, helps you become fully engaged in activities, and creates a greater capacity to deal with adverse events.[50]

TIPS:

- Rather than rehashing the past or stress about the future, try to be aware of the present moment. If there is something that running has taught me, it is to maintain a moment-by-moment awareness of my thoughts, my feelings, my bodily sensations, and my surrounding environment. *Mindfulness* is when we tune into what we are sensing in the present moment.
- Find ways to create space to come down from your worried mind and back.
- Try to implement mindfulness practices throughout the day. Schedule a solo trip (or a trip with your partner or friends if going solo is anxiety-inducing) to recharge your batteries and live in the moment.
- Put it on the calendar. Get out of the house!

Chapter 30: Taking Pen to Paper

"I can shake off everything as I write; my sorrows disappear, my courage is reborn." —Anne Frank

After my race, I was on a *high*. To keep the motivation going, I registered again for the Ottawa Half-Marathon in May 2011, hoping that this time I would train even better to set another personal best. Things were calm on the advocacy front that fall of 2010. Nico had started at the new school and was doing the full day. We didn't hear anything from the teacher or principal and were glad things were finally starting to settle. It seemed that Nico was enjoying his experience at the new school. Although there was not much feedback coming in from the class, we didn't think anything of it, as it's such a busy time of year for teachers.

Nico had gotten his Individualized Education Program (IEP) in October and some important objectives had been discussed with the teacher and specialists (speech pathologist and occupational therapists). We still weren't hearing much, but thought "no news is good news." We weren't being informed about what subjects were being taught or whether Nico had seen the speech therapist and the occupational therapist since the IEP. He never had homework, but they were the experts. After all, this school was one of the best autism schools in our province. We didn't need to worry.

One night, as I was pulling Nico's pajama top over his head, I saw something. A purple mark on his upper arm as if someone had grabbed him. There were also a few scratches on his hand. There had been no note from the teacher. No phone call. Except for some short sentences to request his needs, Nico was still nonverbal and nonconversational. So, he couldn't tell me what happened or how things were at school.

We had also noticed that since starting the new school, Nico had acquired more maladaptive behaviors, like laughing out loud for no reason, spinning, dropping to the ground, having a compulsion to play with strings, etc.

Things were accumulating and Rob and I were starting to get very concerned by the silence surrounding what was going on in this school.

I called the principal. I wanted a face-to-face meeting. I was told she was at a conference and then leaving for Christmas vacation. I would have to wait until the new year. The meeting was set for February.

I kept running to preserve my sanity and manage my chronic stress. And I also had other things on my mind. In October, I had begun to have some vaginal bleeding between periods, no more than some light spotting. In the beginning, I didn't think this was serious as it was just happening occasionally, mostly after my runs. But when the spotting continued even on the days I didn't run, I found this strange.

I contacted the nurse at my medical clinic and she agreed that this was abnormal. She said she would call me back. I hadn't even checked another thing off my list when she did. She had talked to my doctor and had already made an urgent appointment with the gynecologist for early January. She also advised me to schedule an ultrasound as soon as possible. Vaginal bleeding in between periods can have many causes. While some causes may be easy to treat, others can indicate a serious underlying condition, including a hormone imbalance or even cancer.

Obviously, Christmas 2010 was very stressful. When I met with the gynecologist, she was professional, but I could only see the worry in her eyes. She scheduled a curettage and hysteroscopy surgery for the next opening. These procedures allow for the removal of the uterine lining and examination of the tissue under a microscope. We had to make sure bleeding was not due to pre-cancerous cells.

The week before the surgery, my mom came from Ottawa to take care of the kids. The surgery was quick and brought good news: no abnormal cells had been found on the lining of the uterus and moreover I should no longer have any bleeding in between menstrual cycles. If I did, I should call her immediately. I felt relieved and happy. I still had one question for my doctor: How long until I could resume running? She told me that I should take at least a month off before resuming pounding the pavement. At first, I was OK with that. Then I realized that for the first time in a while, I could not rely on running for stress relief.

The day of the meeting arrived. Rob was away on a business trip. Thankfully, I wasn't alone as I had brought Nico's social worker and the local readaptation center's speech therapist who had evaluated Nico's language skills the previous spring. The meeting was conveniently held in Nico's classroom. The principal, teacher, aide, and the school's speech therapist were there. When I asked why the occupational therapist was not present, I was advised that she was not available that day.

I began to inquire about what was going on in the class. The more questions I asked, the more I realized that there was not much teaching going on in this school. Nico had two binders: one for

French and one for math. I asked to look at the binders to see if Nico had made progress since September. The binders were virtually empty with a few token pages for each month. The teacher advised me that this academic year, it had been very difficult to consistently teach French or math. The reason? The kids in Nico's class were much more severe than Nico and they didn't do academics, so the teacher's focus was more on life skills like toilet training.

Yes, toilet training! Something that Nico had been taught when he was three years old. Obviously, neither the teacher nor the aide had much time for anything else. I asked what Nico did while both the teacher and the aide were busy with the other students. They pointed to a corner of the class they named the *coin calme* (the "quiet corner" in English) which had a mat, a rocking chair, and some sensory toys like lamps, strings, shiny objects, collars, all types of stretchy balls . . . what was wrong with this picture? There was not a single book in this area. Not even a basic alphabet book. I was boiling mad. This could not be! They were taking our children's intelligence for granted. I am glad that I had the social worker and the readaptation center's speech therapist with me for emotional support; otherwise, I would have totally lost it at the meeting that day. Yes, our kids have challenging behaviors but they also have untapped intelligence and potential that is just waiting to be uncovered.

These kids cannot be left to their own devices. If you leave Nico or any other kid with classic autism alone without any direction, I can guarantee that they won't do anything functional and will self-stimulate all day. It is guaranteed! And this is what was happening in this class, in this school. What bothered me even more was how nonchalant the teacher and even the principal were. I sensed that the staff had a general disregard to make a difference in the lives of these kids. I was shocked, dumbfounded. This was supposed to be one of the most specialized autism schools in the province and they were treating the students like they couldn't learn anything other than toilet skills! This was a glorified day care!

My exchange with the speech therapist was equally demoralizing. Her tone was condescending and she was on the defensive when I asked her a couple of questions that put her on the spot. I had gone to enough workshops and conferences on speech therapy to know that one of the language strategies she was suggesting was full of c**p. I knew full well that she was taking my son's intelligence for granted almost to the point of being disrespectful. As for the occupational therapist, Nico was supposed to see every month, I was advised that she had only seen Nico once since the beginning of the year.

This was a joke. I almost felt dizzy. I was biting my tongue not to say expletives during the meeting. I just could not bear to hear this nonsense any longer. I told the principal that I would have a separate meeting with my social worker and the speech therapist from the readaptation center, devise a plan of action, and get back to her within the next three days. One thing was clear: things had to change immediately; otherwise, Nico would not be coming back the following school year.

On the way home, I started to cry. Although I was enraged, I think my overwhelming feeling was that of sadness for the way this school was treating these kids and their families. After all the efforts made during the early years trying to get Nico as independent and as functional as possible, the public school system was a catastrophe!

My mom was still in town because of my recent surgery and because Alex's eight birthday was just around the corner. She saw that I had been crying. She hugged me tightly. I told her all about the meeting and she was as sad and mad as me. I put the kids to bed, and as I was about to get my running clothes on to go for a quick jog to relax my mind, I realized that I was still forbidden by the gynecologist to run! I still changed and went for a walk, but what I really wanted at this moment was to pound the pavement. I was *really* craving running that night.

I didn't have my running to hold my hand and tell me that everything was going to be OK. You see, that is how I had come to consider my running: it was and it continues to be my sanctuary. Running is the *me* time that allows me to have those ugly cries, think and strategize for the future, and physically ground myself. Something about the repetition of running is soothing for the soul and the mind. More than ever, I realized how running had saved my sanity that past year and a half.

Three days after the disastrous meeting with the school, I met with Nico's social worker and the readaptation center's speech therapist to devise an action plan for monitoring: (1) what academics were being taught to Nico weekly, (2) what work was being done by the school's speech therapist and occupational therapist, and (3) what life skills were being taught. I forwarded this action plan to the school's principal, thinking that they would be proactive. Instead, the inaction, secrecy, and condescending attitude toward us continued.

Personally, the first two months of 2011 were probably some of the most difficult of my autism journey: (1) my health scare and not knowing for a month whether those cells in my uterus were pre-cancerous, (2) feeling mentally exhausted by the never-ending fight for better services for Nico, (3) not having my running available for my mental release, and (4) Rob not being there for emotional support, as he was travelling for business continually during that period.

Looking back, I now believe that I was *once again* on the verge of a burnout or clinical depression. Though I was functioning properly and taking care of my kids, I was on autopilot.

I felt sorry for my Nico, who had worked so hard up to this point. He had continued to persevere, despite all the obstacles thrown at him. I also felt sorry for my family and for Team Nico. For nearly eight years, everyone had worked every day to make sure that Nico could have a happy and full life, despite his limitations. And now this. I felt lost . . . I was disappointed, sad, mad, incredulous, and heartbroken.

This was the straw that broke the camel's back. Three different schools in four years, three different experiences with the last school being the most disappointing of all—where all Nico was learning was maladaptive behaviors! One of the best autism public schools in the province was grossly underestimating the intelligence and the potential of these kids. With staff who were condescending and disrespectful of parents and worse—of their students. I don't know how I was able to keep it together this time around. If it had not been for the kids, I was on the brink and ready to call it a day.

But somehow, I also knew that there was so much to do in terms of advocacy for these kids and their parents that I *needed* to go on. I believe that apart from the kids, what kept me alive during that time was rage. I vowed that I would not let *anyone underestimate my child's potential ever*. And even though I did not have my running to help me cope with this stress and anxiety, I put the stress to use.

I began writing out absolutely everything that was wrong with this school, the secrecy, the disrespect and condescending attitude of staff, the lack of academic teaching, etc. I began compiling all the complaint letters I had sent to the previous two principals as well as the inaction that followed. I made a list of action items with their corresponding deadlines. The attorney in me was back in full force! At first, this writing was all about mounting a case against the school board. But the more I wrote, the more I found this was helping me with my frustrations and emotions. Eventually, I found solace writing about other topics like my fear for Nico's future or the impact this autism journey was having on Alex. I had a separate notebook where I began to pour all my thoughts and feelings onto paper, not worrying about spelling mistakes or if the sentences made sense. I just wrote and wrote and sometimes wrote and cried and only stopped when I felt like my mind and heart were calm and clear.

Looking back, I realize that unknowingly, I was using writing— or what is called *journaling*—to calm my mind and channel my stress. Research has shown that journaling is a helpful tool in managing stress, anxiety, and depression.[51] It can be a healthy way to express ourselves and can help us clarify our thoughts, deal with overwhelming emotions, and be a good problem-solving tool.[52]

Journaling is a viable option when you don't have the time to use physical stress management techniques like exercise or yoga, for example. Although it doesn't provide you with exercise's feel-good endorphins, journaling is a great practice for managing depression,.[53] overall stress reduction, as well as self-knowledge and emotional healing. When we have a problem and we are stressed, keeping a journal can help us identify what is causing that stress or anxiety. Once we have identified our stressors, we can work on a plan to resolve the problems and reduce the stress.

Since, at that time, I didn't have my running to ground me and anchor me, I used journaling to clarify my ideas and to help me prioritize my concerns. This gave me control and helped me stay on top of my life. More on journaling in my next book.

TIPS:
- **When you don't have an outlet to help you manage stress and anxiety, you must find a way to channel that stress.**
- **Researchers have found that writing and *journaling* can be an effective stress management tool.**
- **Get yourself a journal and start writing everything that comes to mind. Don't worry about spelling mistakes or if what you are writing makes sense. Just**

let those feelings flow. Try to identify what you would like to change and problem solve. From there, write a to-do list and get going.

- Journaling can help you gain control of your emotions and improve your mental health.

Chapter 31: Preserving Longevity and Using Stress as Fuel

"We cannot rid ourselves of stress, but approaching stressful events with a challenge mentality can help promote protective stress reliance in body and in mind." —Dr. Elizabeth Blackburn and Dr. Elissa Epel.

Because of my cancer scare, I began to look for ways to enhance my health apart from exercising. One of the first things that I looked into was improving my nutrition. Thanks to all the running magazines and books I had been reading, my nutrition had vastly improved. But I was looking at ways to make it even better. A couple of days before my surgery, I went to a local Chapters bookstore to look for some health, wellness, and nutrition books to read while recovering from my surgery. I came across the book *Crazy Sexy Diet* by Kris Carr. Faced with a liver cancer diagnosis, Kris made long-lasting lifestyle changes, including changes in her diet, that eventually enabled her to live a full life despite her cancer diagnosis.[54] I bought the book and started reading it the same night.

What struck me most was the foreword by Dr. Dean Ornish, founder and president of the Preventive Medicine Research Institute. In it, he discussed Dr. Elizabeth Blackburn and Dr. Elissa Epel's research, which I mentioned in Part 2, on how chronic emotional stress impacts the enzyme telomerase and shortens telomeres (the DNA-protein complexes at the end of chromosomes that protect against aging). They found that the more stressed the women in their research study felt and the longer they felt stressed, the lower their telomerase and the shorter their telomeres. This, in turn, could lead to premature aging and susceptibility to a myriad of diseases, including cardiovascular disease and cancer. According to Dr. Ornish, this was the first study providing genetic evidence indicating that chronic emotional stress might shorten a woman's lifespan. And guess who Dr. Blackburn et al. used as research subjects likely to record chronic stress throughout their lives. None other than mothers of chronically ill children, including *autism moms*!

These same women—who *must* stay physically healthy and mentally and emotionally strong for their kids—had shorter lifespans because of the insidious chronic stress they were under. This was an eye-opener for me and, at the same time, it corroborated the reality of being an autism mom and a full-time caregiver—the emotional suffering, the hard work, the 24/7 effort, the sacrifice, the chronic stress, the anxiety, the worry about the future. This was *my* life. It had been my life for close to nine years now. And there was a lot more stress to come. All taking a toll on my physical, mental, and emotional health, and now I knew I was in danger of . . . shortening my lifespan! I, Claudia Taboada, autism mom who could not die!

Just thinking about what would happen to Nico when mom and dad are gone is one of the biggest stressors in my life, one that haunts me every single day and keeps me up at night. The overall decline associated with this stress was real, and now this research proved it.

But another facet to this research would have an even bigger impact on me. Dr. Blackburn and Dr. Eppel also found that it wasn't an objective measure of stress that determined the effects on these mothers' telomeres; it was the mother's *perception* of stress that mattered. In other words, the mothers who *perceived* themselves to be under the most stress were the ones with the shortest telomeres. But mothers who had become stress resilient had switched their mindset and, instead of fearing stress, saw it with a challenge mentality. This means that even though we realize that times may be very difficult, we can still shape stress to our purpose or make stress work for us, as when I decided to put all my energy into fighting for Nico's rights for accommodation and a better education or when, early on in our autism journey, I fought for partial public funding for Nico's early intervention program. As Dr. Ornish perfectly stated, "Two women might be in comparable situations, but one had learned to manage her stress better by empowering herself and taking charge."

Research has shown that once we switch our mindset, our body listens.[55] Our physiological responses to stress become healthier, and we find ourselves experiencing more of the positives and less of the negatives associated with stress.[56] Studies have also shown that if channeled properly, stress can have a positive role to play and can be beneficial to our productivity. For instance, it has been shown that manageable stress can (1) increase focus and alertness, (2) sharpen our performance, (3) boost our immune system, and (4) build resilience.[57]

Researchers have also studied something called "post-traumatic growth" when people experience lasting benefits from extremely stressful situations, including: (1) increased appreciation of life, (2) improved relationships with others, (3) new possibilities in life, (4) increased personal strength, and (5) spiritual change.[58]

This is just the tip of the iceberg, and I will expand more about the topics of stress resiliency, the benefits of adopting a challenge mentality, and how to develop an *unstoppable badass mindset* in my next book, *Rediscover the Unstoppable Badass in You: The Busy Women's Guide to Self-Care, Fitness, Stress Management and Living Your Best Life.*

What I do know is that reading the foreword by Dr. Ornish that night was a gift! A gift from above telling me to persevere on this new path of transformation. This new journey that had begun by accident when I first laced up to take Sicas out for a walk back in December 2008 was no fluke. This was the validation that I needed to stay the course. I needed to become stress resilient to extend my life. My main objective was to be around long enough to take care of Nico as an adult. It was essential to keep going and implement any other lifestyle changes that could empower me and preserve those telomeres.

Every time I think about giving up—stopping my exercise regimen, not following up on my medical appointments, getting lazy with my nutrition, cutting too much sleep—I remember my telomeres! I credit this *aha*! moment for playing a role in saving my sanity during those first months of 2011 when I was starting to lose hope.

TIPS:
- **The research has shown that there is an intrinsic link between chronic stress and premature aging.**
- **We must do everything in our power to turn stress into positive stress.**
- **Stress that will become fuel for growth and productivity.**
- **Make a list of activities that you can do to turn your negative stress into positive stress. Can you use your voice to promote acceptance and inclusion for your special needs child in the school system, public health system, or anywhere for that matter? Can you volunteer at a special needs organization? Can you create a charity to help people in need in your area? These are just a few examples, but a myriad of ways are available to turn your stress around and use it as fuel to make an impact in your community.**

Chapter 32: Homeschooling but Taking Steps to Preserve My Self-Care

"I have come to believe that caring for myself is not self-indulgent. Caring for myself is an act of survival." —Audre Lorde

A month after my surgery, I returned to running, and oh, how I had missed it! My ultimate stress reliever! My sanctuary! I was craving this comeback so badly, but I had to be cautious. The first time I attempted to run, I was afraid that I would start bleeding again. but there was no reason to be afraid. Eventually, I eased back into my regular exercise routine.

Because of my lack of training, I had to skip the Ottawa Half-Marathon which was to be held in May. However, I gave myself the objective of competing in two or three half-marathons in August and September and going back to Toronto to run the half-marathon to improve on my finishing time of the previous year.

Nico, was now ten years old and getting bigger and stronger. We had recently discovered that he loved to play the piano and thanks to his teacher Goran, he was developing a passion for the instrument. Thanks to our homeschooling sessions in the afternoon, Nico continued to make steady progress with his reading and he was also learning self-help skills such as making his bed, making easy breakfast (grilled toast, cereal, etc.), doing the laundry. Thanks to Tom's patience, Nico had also become an avid downhill skier. With that said, apart from requesting his needs, Nico was still nonverbal and nonconversational.

Thankfully, we had enough activities at home to keep Nico busy and ensure that he was cognitively stimulated. School was another story. We had the impression that nothing was being done by the staff to nurture Nico's potential and put his intelligence to good use.

Our troubles with the school board persisted for the rest of the year and when summer arrived our decision was made: Nico would not be going back to this school and I would homeschool from now on. We would also be considering filing a complaint against the school board for negligence and for all the grief, anxiety, and stress that the three changes in school had caused our family and, especially, our precious Nico.

TIPS:
- **Don't be afraid to take drastic action where your child is concerned.**
- **Keep documentation of everything and advocate for your child as needed.**
- **You may contact autism organizations in your area to lend a hand and help you with representation before health and education commissions and agencies.**

For the sake of routine, we decided to keep Nico in school until the end of the school year. Only three weeks remained and this would leave me some time to start buying and preparing materials for homeschooling.

Although the thought of homeschooling Nico full time was overwhelming, it was clearly the only good option. Nico's experience in this school had been degrading and demeaned his intelligence and potential—with virtually no academic teaching and lots of maladaptive behaviors picked up along the way. Since I had been Nico's therapist and teacher for a while, I would just continue on the same path.

But this time it would be different. Because of my newfound respect for self-care, I was adamant that we needed to hire extra help for Nico in the form of a tutor or a student in special needs care counseling who would work with Nico and give me some respite. Ideally, the person would work with Nico for a couple of hours a day to work on new skills or generalize what he was learning with me to another setting. We would ask the school board to cover the cost.

So began the quest for the perfect aide or therapist. After a few rounds of interviews and consulting with a couple of autism clinics, we decided that the best option would be to bring Nico to an autism clinic where he could work one-on-one with a therapist and be supervised by an on-site psychologist. The curriculum would be quite comprehensive and would include language, communication, and self-help skills. Nico would go for a couple of hours five times a week in the mornings. This would give him a routine outside of the home and would allow me to keep the exercise routine that was so necessary for my physical and mental health. We would begin these sessions in mid-August.

As for my running, that July my training was complicated by the fact that Nico was particularly anxious. I attributed this increase in anxiety to several factors, the most significant being the last school. Nico started going to his two hours a day Adapted Swim and Gym camp, but he had a hard time, as he's anxiety was getting the best of him. Because of the last school, we noticed an undeniable behavioral regression in which Nico had more autistic behaviors and was now unable to bear any type of sensory stimulation. This is turn made him anxious and prone to aggressive outbursts (scratching others, pulling hair, or forcefully grabbing people's arms) at a drop of a hat. A few times a week, I had to pick Nico up before the end of the session because he had trouble calming down and relaxing.

By mid-August, Nico started going to the autism clinic. It was a two-hour block and I had to drop him off and pick him up. In total, I had about one hour and fifteen minutes to myself . . . and it was absolutely glorious! I used that precious time to run. Two days I would run forty-five minutes, two days I would run for an hour, all easy. At the time, I still had no coach. My rationale was that I was using this me time as my mental health fix while building my base to run the upcoming half-marathons.

Nico seemed to like his new routine and his new therapist. He would go to the autism clinic in the morning and then we would do activities and some academics in the afternoon.

Faced with the situation where I had to become Nico's full-time caregiver, I saw the specter of losing my identity *once again.* Because I knew now the value of self-care and self-preservation, I was no longer willing to compromise my wellbeing. Hence my insistence for a therapist, educator, or tutor to work with Nico and provide me some respite. I was resolved to *make time for me.* I continued to run, eat well and hydrate regularly, sleep at least six hours per night, do some meditation, and journal my thoughts. And I continued to race. And as we will see more in detail in Part 4, racing became an essential ingredient in my toolbox by transforming my mindset and empowering me to think big.

TIPS:
- **I keep insisting, but you need to do all you can to have some daily respite.**
- **Ask someone to care for your child while you take time for you (even if it's just to go for a twenty-minute walk around the block or to go to the grocery store *alone*).**

Chapter 33: Top of the List

In late October, we had some unexpected good news. Years ago, we had put Nico on a waiting list for a private autism school in Montréal. With all we were going through, I had forgotten that Nico was still on the waiting list, and he was now at the top.

We didn't know what to think. We had put a lot of effort into refining our homeschooling program and knew we were on the right track. But we also wanted Nico to see more people and become accustomed to all kinds of sensory stimulation. This school had an excellent reputation in the autism community. We knew we couldn't pass up this opportunity. It was now or never.

By mid-November, Nico became a student at this new school. Our new mission became to help Nico integrate as successfully as possible. And although, at the time, we decided not to pursue our complaint against the public school board, we advised them that if ever things were not to work out in this new school, we would go back to homeschooling Nico and request they pay for a part-time tutor for the remaining years of his schooling.

Nico seemed comfortable in the new school, and for the first time since his diagnosis, we were finally able to *breathe*.

Having a school where your child's intelligence and potential are not underestimated is a gift. The same can be said for a school where there is cooperation between parents, staff, and school management. Not having to constantly fight for your child's right for a good primary and secondary education was a huge weight off our shoulders.

Of course, I was still under chronic stress, but less so than in the previous years. Special needs parents are *always* under chronic stress. It comes from the day-to-day caregiving that keeps us in a state of fight or flight *all the time*. It's a feeling of constant vigilance and urgency, which makes it difficult for us to completely relax.

In addition, as I explained in previous chapters, a bigger and darker cloud always hovers over every special needs parent whom I've met: the fear of the future for our child once they reach adulthood. While running was doing an excellent job at keeping me in the present most days, when Nico was more anxious, had more difficult behaviors, or bad days at school, my fear for the future would return full force. So, even though Nico was finally in a school that accepted him and challenged him academically, I had to make sure that *I kept up with my exercise regimen as well as my other self-care tools.* By then, I knew that it was necessary to preserve my physical, mental, and emotional health and to have the energy and stamina to take care of Nico well into his adult years.

TIPS:
- **Always keep searching for what is best for your child.**
- **As parents, you are the ones who know their strengths better than anybody else. Do not let anyone underestimate your child's potential, *ever*.**
- **Sometimes, homeschooling may be the best option for your child. And if this is the case, it is imperative that as a primary caregiver, you take the steps to preserve your physical and mental wellness. Even if you**

manage to find the right school set up for your child and things ease up, you *must keep making self-care a priority*.

- Special needs parenting is a *long-term contract,* so you must stay the course to preserve your health and longevity.

Chapter 34: Acceptance

"When we truly embrace acceptance, that's when our body exhales and can begin healing." —Kris Carr

When Nico started in this new school, I had an overwhelming sense of gratitude toward the staff, who, despite the multiple behaviors of these kids, including aggression, were so devoted and always searching for ways to challenge the children and bring out their potential. Not having to deal with the public school board and its draining and toxic effects on my mental health, I now had more time to focus on what was important: Nico's future and my own *acceptance* of his condition. I had to admit to myself that I hadn't fully accepted Nico's autism.

Looking back, I believe that for the first six years of my family's autism journey, I was still in the denial mindset. I still believed that one day, Nico would be miraculously "cured of his autism," despite having a document stating in no uncertain terms that he has classic autism as well as an intellectual delay. Even when we had huge setbacks with inclusion in regular classrooms—at the preschool and at the first public school—I still believed that this autism thing would go away with time and that we would live happily ever after. I continued to search frantically for any cures, treatments, methods, or answers that would take away his autistic traits and make him "more normal." As Nico could not handle the routine nor the constant sensory stimulation in regular classrooms, I began to realize that this was more than just a passing condition. Eventually, I surrendered. I accepted that Nico's autism would not go away. I accepted that it was part of Nico's being. I accepted that this was a long-term condition and not a disease that you can cure by taking drugs, following a medical treatment, or even a 40h/week intervention program. *I finally had to accept that my autistic boy would become an autistic adult.* And because of the severity of his autism, Nico would become an autistic adult who would not be able to go to university, get married, or have an independent life. Nico would likely be dependent on others for the rest of his life. This was a huge step in my healing process. Probably the biggest . . . a huge weight off my shoulders.

This realization changed me. From now, on my mission would be to ensure that my boy would have a future where, despite his autism, he would thrive and become a contributing member of society. *My acceptance* would enable me to find my voice, fight for his rights and for his future, and advocate for autism acceptance and rights for those who don't have many rights to begin with—*adults with autism.*

If I had to pinpoint what exactly opened my eyes to the reality of Nico's autism, I would have to say that it was listening to and reading the works of autistic individuals like Dr. Temple Grandin and Québec's own Brigitte Harrison. Dr. Grandin, a professor of animal science at Colorado State University, has a PhD in animal science from the University of Illinois and has designed one-third of all the livestock-handling facilities in the US and other countries. Being one of the first people on the spectrum to publicly share personal insights, she is *the* ultimate autism spokesperson and expert. She has written several books and gives lectures and conferences all over the world about autism.

Brigitte Harrison is a social worker, an expert on autism spectrum disorder, and an autistic person herself. She co-founded Concept ConsulTED Inc. in 2016, which has since become the SACCADE *Centre D'Expertise en Autisme* (Centre for Autism Expertise) in Québec City. She is also the co-creator of the SACCADE Conceptual Language Model[59] and is co-author of the book *New Ways of Understanding Autism.*[60]

I first discovered Dr. Grandin when I read *Thinking in Pictures: My Life with Autism.*[61] Reading her book would profoundly change my perception of autism as well as the way I saw my child. For the first time in my family's journey, I had a new viewpoint about my son's autism. What Dr. Grandin has told the world is simple: our autistic kiddos are "different, not less."[62] This was an entirely new mindset that allowed me to see Nico not as someone with a disability but as someone with a *different* set of abilities and talents that needed to be nurtured. I went from someone who desperately wanted to "save Nico from his autism" and try to "change him" to someone who *accepted* him as he was: with all his challenges but also with his *unique strengths.*

And, yes, I continued and still continue to search for therapies, but the objective has shifted from trying to cure him to trying to make him more independent and help him better adapt and function in a society that is not very accepting of differences. I finally allowed myself to say, "Yes, Nico is autistic—severely autistic—and he will probably remain severely autistic for the rest of his life." Instead of trying to make Nico into someone he isn't, my goal became for him to be a fulfilled autistic individual who, despite his limitations, will thrive by fully developing his character, unique abilities, and talents.

Dr. Grandin has also said that in autism, and presumably in other long-term conditions, "there needs to be an emphasis on what a child *can do* instead of what they cannot do."[63] This inspired us as a family to shift our focus and energy from working on things that were too difficult or impossible for Nico to finding passions for him. So instead of "getting rid of his autism," our focus as a family became let's find something that Nico likes, try to encourage him in that direction, and see if he sticks with it. With a lot of patience and perseverance from us parents and some wonderful teachers and mentors who have believed in him along the way, Nico is now able to play the piano, downhill ski, and go for long bike rides with his dad.

Finally, Dr. Grandin also said, "It is never too late to expand the mind of a person on the autism spectrum."[64] This means that thanks to brain neuroplasticity, people on the autism spectrum continue to learn even into adulthood.

This has fueled my inner fire to seek a better future for my son. I fight for conditions that will enable my boy to flourish as an autistic adult. I want to increase access to educational and training opportunities, create better housing, have more options for leisure activities, etc. And it all begins with spreading awareness and shining a light on the problem so the general population and governments around the world can understand where parents of special needs children stand.

TIPS:
- **Regardless of where you are in your journey, it is important to come to terms with the fact that your special needs child will become a special needs adult.**
- **This acceptance doesn't mean that you will abandon the fight.**
- **This acceptance can allow you to shift priorities and focus your energy on new goals for your child and your family.**
- **Read books written by autistic individuals. I've mentioned those by Dr. Temple Grandin and Brigitte Harrison, but a myriad of books have been written by autistic adults that will enlighten you about the condition, give you tips, help you cope, and, most importantly, *give you hope* for the future.**

Claudia Taboada

PART 4: Running, Racing, and Becoming an *Unstoppable Badass*

Claudia Taboada

Chapter 35: Marathon Momma

"Two roads diverged in a wood, and I—I took the one less traveled by, and that has made all the difference." —Robert Frost

Because running and racing had now become an integral part of my self-care toolbox, I kept at it. In the summer and fall of 2011, I was back at homeschooling Nico full-time and I needed a mental break from the daily routine. I wanted to do something out of the ordinary, something *epic*. With me back at the driving seat of Nico's program, I feared losing my identity once more. I feared going back to living on autopilot and losing myself in the whirlwind. And for that reason, I felt the need to step out of my comfort zone and challenge myself physically and mentally. I wanted to keep reminding myself that I could do hard things and I wanted to preserve the challenge mentality—or what I now call the *badass mindset*—that had slowly re-emerged from the ashes of hopelessness and despair.

The year prior, I had registered for the Toronto Half-Marathon. Initially, I wanted to go for a half-marathon PB (personal best) and crush the one I had obtained the previous year in Toronto. But I knew I didn't have enough time to improve my time from 2010. So, the next obvious epic goal for me was... to run the marathon (42.2 kms or 26.2 miles)! I, therefore, switched my registration from the half-marathon to the marathon, and I didn't tell anyone, not even Rob. Everyone thought that I was running the half!

Of course, I didn't expect to finish the marathon and even planned on bringing some money with me to take a cab if ever I had to abandon mid-race. All I really wanted to see was how far I could push this body of mine. My longest runs to date had been half-marathons (21.1 kms or 13.1 miles) and I didn't really have time to ramp up my mileage.

Running my first marathon was an unforgettable and priceless experience. And I finished—without injuries and with a stronger mindset. From all the cherished memories, two stand out the most.

The first one happened on race morning. As I was pinning my bib in front of the mirror, I remembered the following words by the late Steve Jobs, "If today were the last day of my life, would I want to do what I am about to do today?" And my answer at that moment was a resounding and unequivocal "*Hell freaking yesssss!*"

The second priceless memory is another epiphany in my journey of transformation. It has become a guiding principle for the way I've decided to live my life from now on, despite the cards that I have been dealt with. And it has empowered me ever since to take risks in my choices with Nico and in my personal life. At around the 20 km mark of this race, the course bifurcates. The half-marathon runners turn to the left and run another 1.1 km to the finish line. The marathon runners turn to the right and continue to the Toronto waterfront, an industrial area, the Beaches neighborhood, and so on. As I was approaching the 20 km mark, I had to make a decision: either turn to the left and go with the half-marathon runners or *follow the road less traveled*— that of the marathon runners. I had not trained for the marathon.

I still had the choice to abandon my marathon idea, turn left and go with the half-marathon runners. *But I didn't.*

I remember toying with the idea for a few minutes, and then I decided that *today was the day*! I would be the one who would attempt to run a marathon without running no more than 21 kms in her life. As the saying goes, "I didn't come this far to only come this far." I *had no interest in turning to the left. This was it.* I still remember the exact song that was playing at the moment I made my decision: "I will survive" by Gloria Gaynor. Unbelievable but true. Here I was, during one of the most important moments of my transformational journey listening to this women empowerment anthem! I believe that it was a sign from above telling me to be a *fearless badass* and *just go for it.* And I did with every inch of my body and soul. I freaking did, and I was so damn proud of myself when I crossed that finish line.

I ran this race with heart and I could not have been more pleased with the experience. I ran continuously until 34 kms and then alternated walking and running to finish. In awe of my body once more, I collected the medal I had coveted the year prior in the hotel lobby.

I was overjoyed! This was a *celebration of life* and of having survived the spring of 2011—one of the most challenging periods in our family's autism journey. And I believe that the reason I chose the "road less traveled" was because my mindset was ready to take the leap, to take the risk. The *badass mindset* was now guiding me and showing me the way. This decision would be key to my growth and to my transformational journey. The feeling of empowerment, fulfillment, and self-efficacy I got from running my first marathon was second to none.

After recovering from the marathon, I decided to add a few more items to my self-care toolbox: Meditation, Epsom salt baths, and Bikram Yoga (a ninety-minute class consisting of a series of twenty-six exercises in a room heated to 35–42°C). I would try to do at least one session of Bikram Yoga per week and try to schedule it after my long run to relieve sore muscles. And as I will describe more in detail in my next book, yoga and meditation have become important components of my self-care, as have Epsom salt baths. The three allow me to relax my body and mind. I have even crafted a fifteen-minute yoga routine that I do every day religiously before I go to bed. I also seek to practice meditation daily to seek stillness and soothe the mind. As for the Epsom salt baths, I do them when I can, usually after long runs or early in the morning before everyone wakes up.

TIPS:
- **Sometimes, we need to take the road less traveled to rediscover our strength.**
- **Smart risk-taking promotes a growth mindset.**
- **Within your passion/self-care activity, try to set a big enough goal that makes you scared but excited at the same time. Take the risk and go for it.**
- **And what if you fail? Making mistakes and learning from them is one of the major keys to success.**
- **Keep going! And don't feel like you have to run a marathon to feel empowered. Anything that takes you out of your comfort zone can do the trick! Play guitar, do an open mic, do flamenco dancing, or go out and try some hip-hop dancing instead. Don't be afraid to up the ante, to try, and to fail.**

Chapter 36: Racing for Autism Awareness and Acceptance

"As you grow older, you will discover that you have two hands, one for helping yourself, the other for helping others."
—Maya Angelou

A few weeks after I completed my first marathon, Nico would begin a new adventure at the school that would become his home away from home until this day. Filled with gratitude toward this school and its staff, I wanted to give back and I approached the school's director of fundraising with an initiative. At the time, I had already done three marathons (Toronto 2011, Ottawa 2012, and Toronto 2012). At each race, I had seen people wearing T-shirts of foundations and organizations raising funds for different causes. I knew that in Montréal, a race was scheduled in April called the Scotiabank Charity Challenge. Organizations would build fundraising teams to raise money and spread awareness at the same time.

So, I put the two and two together: my passion for running and my passion for autism acceptance to suggest this fundraising initiative. We joined the challenge in the spring 2013 and over the years, we've raised over $100,000 for the school, even winning the Charity Challenge in 2014. This was and continues to be a great spring tradition that unifies parents and staff, raises funds for the operating costs of the school, and promotes autism awareness and acceptance in the Montréal area.

As for my athletic endeavors from 2012 to 2016, I continued to run and race as I had been. I kept running four times a week, with most of these miles being very easy. On the days I didn't run, I would cross train with Pilates. Before meeting my first running coach in 2016, I found no reason to get a coach. I truly enjoyed coaching myself during that period. It allowed me to learn and discover things on my own without the pressure of performing for personal bests or for records.

Each year, I read books and found new ways to challenge myself. I enjoyed books by Christopher McDougall, George A. Sheehan, Amby Burfoot, Matt Fitzgerald, etc. I also read biographies of some running legends. Each training cycle, I would focus on something new. For instance, in the summer and fall of 2013, I focused on my speed by incorporating more interval training, and I improved my times on the 5K, 10K, and marathon. In 2014, I focused on improving my cadence. In 2015, I decided to build a strong aerobic base and got my body to burn fat for fuel by running for a full year under a 138 bpm heart rate. And the list goes on . . .

I kept learning, discovering, analyzing, and experimenting with my own body. Yes! I was becoming an expert and enjoyed geeking out over this activity that not only had given me back my life but *made me feel so alive every time I laced up*! At the time, I was just enjoying learning about this passion of mine, never really aspiring to become a faster runner.

During those years, Rob increased the frequency of his work travel, often going for weeks of back-to-back traveling, and it was tough on me and the kids. But since he was racking up the air miles, we made a pact that at least twice per year, I would go off to a new country to run a marathon to have a mommy break and some *me* time. Most of my race trips have been solo. And although they have been short (a weekend or four–five days at the most) they became an essential item of my self-preservation toolbox and a means of self-growth. There is nothing more empowering than traveling solo in a new country where you don't know the language and you have to make sure that your logistics are on point so that you can run a marathon two days after you arrive!

So, from May 2012 to April 2016, I ran countless half-marathons and fourteen marathons, including two in my hometown of Montréal, two in Toronto, and two in Ottawa. And I also developed a passion for traveling to run marathons, something that I still try to do at least once a year. So, from spring 2013 to spring 2016, I ran five marathons in Europe (Barcelona, Nice-Cannes, Rome, Athens, and Lisbon) and three in the US (San Francisco, San Diego, and Big Sur). Most of the time, I would race to fundraise and shine a light on the autism condition and the plight of autism families around the world.

In the spring of 2015, I also performed an endurance event that makes me proud to this day: I ran two marathons in eight days (the Ottawa Marathon and the San Diego Marathon) for the organization Autism Speaks Canada. This act of madness allowed me to raise funds for an organization close to my heart as well as become a member of the exclusive worldwide organization, aptly named Marathon Maniacs. I didn't have any injuries after this challenge and this confirmed to me that my strength was endurance events.

I had the endurance; now it was time to get the speed.

TIPS:
- **Volunteering or giving back helps counteract the effects of stress and anxiety and can have a positive impact on our overall psychological well-being.**

- **Make time in your busy schedule to give back and volunteer. By taking time to serve others, you'll feel a sense of meaning and appreciation.**
- **If you can combine both your self-care activity with your passion for helping others, the sense of satisfaction is amplified.**

Chapter 37: Dreaming Big

"Set a goal so big that you can't achieve it until you grow into the person who can." —unknown

The Quest for the Six Star Medal

The Abbott World Marathon Majors are a series of six of the largest and most prestigious marathons in the world: Tokyo, Boston, London, Berlin, Chicago, and New York City. Global health care company Abbott became the official sponsor in 2015. The Six Star Medal, the *most* coveted of all marathon medals, made its debut at the Tokyo Marathon in 2016. Sometime in 2016, this medal became the object of my affection.

My Abbott World Marathons Major journey began the day I ran my fifteenth marathon in Big Sur California in April 2016. On that fateful day, I sat beside an older woman named Esther on the bus to the starting line. Esther was an experienced marathoner and triathlete, with several Boston Marathons and full Ironmans under her belt. We started chatting and when the subject of my training (or rather my lack of training) was brought up, Esther basically gave me sh** for "wasting my potential" and being nonchalant about my training. She thought that I had incredible endurance as I hadn't had a single injury even though my marathon training had been, at best, intermittent and, at worst, nonexistent.

She literally could not believe that I had survived the injury train and thought I had potential for more . . . *way more*. Esther suggested that I join a running club, hire a coach, or do both to see if I could qualify for the Boston Marathon. To do that, you need a qualifying time from another marathon. It hadn't even occurred to me to try. To say that you qualified for Boston is a badge of honor for any runner.

While I was interested, I wondered how this autism mom, who was running mainly to preserve her sanity and to escape from the daily autism whirlwind, could even *dare* to think that she could qualify for one of the most prestigious marathons in the world. Up-to that point in my running journey, being a "speedy" runner let alone "qualifying for Boston" was not on my radar. I loved traveling and running marathons but I did not like *to train properly and consistently* for them. Although I had followed training programs in magazines and books, I did so sporadically and I would get either bored or unmotivated to follow through. I loved running but doing the long runs, intervals, and tempo runs consistently to become a faster marathoner was just not my cup of tea up to that point. And I knew full well that I was lucky not to get injured while doing the bare minimum.

So, when Esther gave me sh**, I knew that she was right. Right then and there, I decided that enough was enough! I owed it to myself to train properly and see how far I could go. But to do so, I needed yet another *epic* goal. A big enough goal that would light my competitive fire and motivate me to train consistently. So, while climbing up the Big Sur hills, I made the decision to complete the six Abbott World Marathon Majors (Berlin, New York, London, Tokyo, Chicago, and Boston) in less than three years. This would force me to get my act together and train hard to qualify for the Boston Marathon if I wanted to finish all six and get the medal of all medals—the Six Star Medal. From now on, I would treat the marathon distance with the respect it deserved and train accordingly.

After Big Sur, I came back to Montréal excited and energized and with a newfound appreciation for training. First item on the list was to find my first Abbott World Marathon Major to run in 2016. Because the six major marathons are in high demand, the organizers have established a lottery system for all except Boston. The only lottery still open was for New York City. I knew it was statistically very unlikely I'd get in, so I went for the Berlin Marathon where I could get a bib via a marathon travel agency. A few weeks later, I found out that I had gotten into NYC via the lottery! So, I would end up running the Berlin Marathon in September 2016 and the New York City Marathon in early November—two Majors in less than six weeks. I was ecstatic!

The second item on the list was to follow Esther's advice and either find a running group, a coach, or both. In the past, I had tried one or two online coaches, and I never followed through, so I knew that I had to have someone local who would hold me accountable. It just so happened that two days after I got into NYC, I saw a Facebook post about a running group in the city of Blainville, in the outskirts of Montréal. I sent an email to the person in charge to give him some information about my running. In the email, I wrote that although I had completed fifteen marathons, I did not consider myself a real marathoner because I didn't know how to train properly. I also said that I wanted to break the four-hour mark at the marathon distance and I was determined to put in the work.

I immediately got an email back from Pierre, who was the coach of this group and who wrote in no uncertain terms that: 1) I had more experience than the average runner and 2) it is the *motivation* that counts. It turned out that this Pierre guy, was Pierre Léveillé, owner of the running store Boutique Endurance where I had been buying my running shoes for years. He is a 1984 Olympian in the 400m hurdles and is also a very well-respected personality in the Québec running community. We talked on the phone and he explained to me his training philosophy and what I needed to do to get faster.

It took me a full two months to call him back. I hesitated because I didn't believe that I had the running talent to follow his training program. And even though I was motivated to train properly and bring my running to the next level, I didn't have the confidence in myself or the belief that I could pull off such a program. Finally, one day on vacation, after one amazing run by the beach and still on a runners' high, I decided to call Pierre back. I had to at least *try*.

Pierre not only gave me the discipline I needed but also was patient enough to teach me the basics of marathon training 101. He also made it very clear that if I wanted results, I needed to focus on quality versus quantity. Except for the Berlin and New York City Marathons for which I had already registered, there would be no more back-to-back marathons in the same season. No more four marathons per year as I had been doing the previous couple of years. There would be one marathon in the spring and one in the fall at the most, with a couple of shorter races in the lead up to these marathons. That's it. Otherwise, he would not coach me. Reluctantly, I agreed and thus began the quest for the coveted Six Star Medal. I began training for the Berlin Marathon in the middle of July 2016. Slowly but surely, I incorporated long runs, intervals, and tempo runs into my routine and did them consistently week after week.

My first goal in my quest was to run a marathon in under four hours. Up until then, my fastest marathon time had been four hours eighteen minutes. Berlin would be my first attempt and New York my second. I didn't achieve sub-four then, but I kept at it. Then, at the London Marathon in April 2017, the real breakthrough happened: I ran a four-hour four-minute marathon with a fourteen-minute personal best with me feeling in control of my race from A to Z. I suspected a good result as two weeks prior, I had a two-minute personal best at a local 10K race. According to Coach Pierre, the London Marathon has been one of my best races ever, and I agree.

Qualifying for the Boston Marathon and training for it

However, I was still waiting for that elusive sub-four marathon. I took only a couple of weeks off after London and resumed my training. On May 9, 2017, one day before Nico's sixteenth birthday, I suffered one of the greatest tragedies of my life. My mom Leticia—whom I adored and who had been a pillar of strength throughout my family's autism journey—passed away unexpectedly from a heart attack.

She had just sold her house in Ottawa to move to Montréal and be closer to her two grandchildren. She moved in November 2016 and passed away the following May. I was *devastated*. But I did not fall apart. I credit my running for keeping me sane during that period and enabling me to weather the storm. I ran and cried my eyes out. In fact, the months of May and June, I cried nearly every time I was out there pounding the pavement. And I would come home calmer and mentally ready for the day ahead.

And I continued to train. This time, Coach Pierre and I were shooting for a sub-four marathon in the fall of 2017. I was determined and knew that if I continued to believe and work hard, that sub-four and eventually that BQ (or in runners' speak, that Boston Qualifying time) would come. Finally, on November 4, 2017, in California, I got another eleven-minute personal best and I qualified for Boston with a six-minute twenty-second cushion. I never cried after marathons until that day.

The Tokyo Marathon and the Chicago Marathon would be next in 2018 and saving the best for last: the iconic Boston Marathon in 2019, for which I had decided to run my best marathon time ever. This would give me a reason to bring my running to the next level. Coach Pierre had suggested that I contact coach Dorys

Langlois, one of the most respected marathon coaches in Montréal. His marathon program is known for being hard and combines both intensity and very high mileage. I hesitated a bit but not for long, as I knew that this was yet another step in my transformational journey.

I met with coach Dorys in early November 2018. He, Pierre, and Esther had stressed to me the fact that joining a running group was beneficial not only for motivation but to help us push hard during those tough speed sessions. I had declined to join these groups in the past because I thought that I was not fast enough and didn't want to make a fool of myself in front of all these speedsters.

But there would be no more hesitation. I was determined to deal with my imposter syndrome head-on. I was a runner damn it! A real runner. I was now mentally ready to become the runner I was always meant to be. So, the stage was set: not only I would be doing coach Dorys' running program but I would also be joining the running group and train with them twice a week for speed sessions at the McGill University track.

To my surprise, not only did I adapt fairly quickly to the program, but I came to truly enjoy my speed sessions with the group—whom I affectionately call my "DDD gang" (for Discipline, Distance and Determination). They welcomed me with open arms. They were and have been very supportive and motivating. And the inspiration I've gotten by observing my faster and more experienced teammates pour everything they have into a workout is definitely second to none. Add to this the camaraderie and sense of belonging, I would not trade this experience for the world! This is my weekly shot of inspiration and I always look forward to suffering with a smile along with my DDD peeps. If you want to get into running, are a relatively new runner or, like me, are an experienced runner who wants to get faster, I would encourage you to join a running club. It will change your life as it has changed mine.

TIPS:

- Pick your tribe wisely. Don't waste your energy on people who drain you with drama and negativity. Go for those who inspire you, motivate you, and push you to be better and make you hungry for life.
- Look for groups or organizations in your community focused on things that matter to you. Join a running group, autism awareness and acceptance organization, a group for painters, or yoga enthusiasts . . . the possibilities are endless.

Boston ended up being one of my toughest marathons to date. Not only it is a very hilly marathon but that year, the conditions were unusually hot and humid. I was on pace until 15K, and then I started to slow down, and after 25K, it was all about survival. At 32K at the infamous Heartbreak Hill, I had a cramp in my leg but didn't walk. I ran all those hills. And I tried to finish with a sprint and smile because after that finish line, I would collect not one but two medals, including *the* medal of all marathon medals—the World Marathon Majors Six Star Medal.

And what an emotional moment it was to finally receive that medal. This journey had started with Sicas ten years earlier. The dream was sparked by Esther and shaped by two coaches who believed in me and gave me the tools I needed to fully exploit my potential. All the training—the early mornings, long runs at +40°C and at -33°C, blisters, effort, and perseverance of this marathon journey were encapsulated in this big shiny medal!

TIPS:

- Don't be afraid to *dream big*. Chase the big dreams that will challenge and transform you. But make sure to set small measurable goals to anchor those dreams. Once you set those goals, your discipline, consistency, and hard work will make those dreams a reality.

- **Start looking for a dream that excites you and scares you at the same time.**
- **Make a plan and set some short-term and long-term goals. Write it all down. Goals help you make decisions.**
- **Look for a coach, a mentor, or like-minded person who will assist you, encourage you, and help you achieve that dream.**

Becoming a Triathlete

In between these marathons, I also decided to push my limits by registering for and training for a triathlon—IRONMAN 70.3 Mont-Tremblant 2018 (consisting of a 1.9 km swim, 90 km bike, 21 km run). I wanted to go beyond my comfort zone by learning how to ride a road bike and swim almost from scratch.

But my triathlon dream was almost not meant to be. On the day of the race, I did the 1.9 km swim in Lake Tremblant and then as I was getting out of the water my left foot hit a big rock and I ended up breaking my middle toe. I still completed the very hilly 90 km bike course with a broken toe. After getting my toe taped at the medical tent, I was hopeful that I would be able to run the 21.1 km or at least walk it. . . . I tried to run but couldn't. So, I walked, but the pain was unbearable and I had to stop at around 3 km. I ended up not finishing the race. I was mad. Mad at the universe for missing my finish line moment by a stupid freak accident. Because of the broken toe, I ended up not running for a full two months.

But everything happens for a reason. Not only did I discover how resilient and mentally strong I had become since Nico's diagnosis but I took advantage of this time off running to become a better cyclist and swimmer. This incident also reignited a new fire in me. I vowed to come back in 2019 with a vengeance. And that's what I did.

After receiving my Six Star Medal in Boston in April 2019, I hesitated to come back to triathlon. IRONMAN 70.3 Tremblant was just two months away. I didn't have enough time to train. My bike was broken. I had to start the swim and bike training over again. It was risky… but that finish line was taunting me.

And I knew I had nothing to lose. I was determined to train as if I were going to race this thing. "If a week before I don't feel I can do it, I won't race. But from now on, I'm giving it all I've got," I told myself in no uncertain terms.

I began to swim three times a week for thirty to forty-five minutes, rode three times a week (two faster rides of about an hour each and one three-hour ride on Fridays). This was on top of following Coach Dory's marathon training plan to a T. On the week leading up to the event, I was still unsure whether or not I would race. Finally, after a particularly reassuring open water training swim in Lake Tremblant four days before the race, I decided to go for it. I was ready.

On the day of the race, I saw my friends, Stephanie and Marie-France, at the swim start. They were instrumental in encouraging me to race and calmed my fears that morning.

"Feel the fear and do it anyway," I kept repeating to myself as I began to swim, particularly as I was making my way toward the deepest water, just before turning around the farthest buoy. And I thought about my mom who had been so proud and supportive of all my athletic endeavors. I felt her with me, protecting me. The water in this area was extremely choppy, and I remember being followed very closely by one of the safety kayaks. I was scared, I was anxious. My heart was racing. I kept asking myself "What the f**k am I doing here?!" But there was also a little voice telling me to stay strong and persevere. I kept swimming furiously until I made it to shore. I still remember my friend Stephanie's face when she saw me after I got out of the water. She was so relieved that I was alive!

I got to the transition area, changed, ate a protein bar, put on my cycling shoes, and then I was off on the bike. I took it easy for the first 15 kms and then I just went for it like a maniac! I must have passed at least two hundred people and I just kept at it, as fast as I could. I prayed that I wouldn't get a flat tire, as I had no idea how to fix a flat.

I finished the bike, had another bar, and then it was off to run the half-marathon. And boy was I grateful to finally get to run. I went at it as if Brad Pitt were waiting for me at the finish line! I was slow but steady and I kept passing runners. I didn't walk once. Again, I passed about another one hundred people if not more. As I was approaching the finish line, I let out a huge victory scream and looked up to the sky. This triathlon was for my mom.

I felt *invincible*. The *badass was now fully back*!

This was the *comeback* that I had dreamt off.

TIPS:
- **When life knocks you down, it's testing you to see whether you have the mental strength to accept your fate, move on, and keep chasing your dreams with a renewed purpose.**
- **As the saying goes, "Every setback is a set up for a comeback."**
- **If you have a setback, switch your mindset. Consider it an opportunity to grow and acquire a new perspective. The comeback will be so much sweeter!**

Chapter 38: Self-Fulfillment and My Second Act

"Be an *unstoppable* badass every day." —Claudia Taboada

I believe that when we get caught up in the caregiving whirlwind or any type of chronic stressful situation, we lose the ability to reach within ourselves and evaluate where our life is at and where it's going. We slowly but surely drift away from our own sense of self until, one day, we no longer recognize *who* we are, what our *goals* are, what our *purpose* is, and what our *mission* in life is.

We just live life from one stressful event to the next without paying attention. We not only forget about our basic needs but by doing so, we rob ourselves from reaching the next level of personal growth, which is the fulfillment of our full potential.

My transformational journey, which first began by finding a passion by accident and sticking with it, eventually led to two realizations: (1) that I needed to take care of my physical, mental, and emotional health and (2) that I could do hard things. These then led to a subsequent switch in mindset—the *badass mindset*—which allowed me to *think big*.

Burnout to Unstoppable

Pushing me to seek *personal growth* and *self-fulfillment* in other areas of my life, this mindset shift has helped me fearlessly embark on my book writing projects, create an activewear line to empower and inspire, and start a transformational life coaching and motivational speaker business.

This is my *second act*. My *reinvention*. My *full transformation* from the overwhelmed autism mom who less than eleven years ago didn't know who she was anymore to the vibrant, passionate, and *unstoppable badass* she has now become.

My *spark* has now been fully reignited and I will not settle for anything less than reaching my maximum potential in all areas of my life.

This a story about overcoming, coping, and transforming. It is the story of how I tapped into my passion, made space for self-awareness, and reclaimed my identity. It is the story of how I found the self-care and stress resiliency tools to better cope and give me the vitality and longevity to care for my Nico well into his adult years. Finally, it is the story of how I rediscovered my spark, my inner power, and the *unstoppable badass* in me.

Afterword

Nico just turned eighteen in May of this year. He continues to go to the same private school for autistic children that he's been going to since November 2011. And I cannot say enough about this school and its staff who, despite their student's severe challenges, continue to support and nurture their talents and potential. This is Nico's home away from home where he feels safe and accepted and where his intelligence is not underestimated. In this school, Nico has made great strides in all aspects of his development. Two years ago, he even began a once-a-week work placement at an office where he shreds paper, files documents, and does other clerical jobs under the supervision and guidance of a trusted educator. Nico can read and type in French and is now learning English. And as we mentioned earlier, Nico has now become an avid downhill skier and loves doing long bike rides with his dad. But most importantly, Nico has found a passion—playing the piano. Thanks to his teacher Goran who has been incredibly patient and encouraging, Nico is now able to read the notes and play the piano flawlessly. However, Nico remains severely autistic and minimally verbal (able to make short sentences to request his needs, but nonconversational). He also continues to be very hypersensitive to loud and sudden noises which can cause severe anxiety.

As for Alex, he is now sixteen and has turned into quite the musician himself. He plays several instruments including the clarinet, the flute, the saxophone, and the bassoon. Alex plays with his school's jazz band and will be finishing high school this year. He is smart, very independent, and someone with a very generous heart who protects and loves his brother Nico unconditionally.

Nico turning eighteen this year spurred me into action. It was one of the main reasons I wrote this book. You see, when you have a neurotypical child, the eighteen-year-old milestone is celebrated. It is a symbol of your child becoming an adult, ready to take on some new responsibilities like going to college, moving out of the family home, getting a job, etc.

For parents of special needs children, eighteen is approached with *apprehension, fear,* and *anxiety.* It's like your child and your family are about to fall into the abyss or as another autism mom has called this—into "the *black hole.*" Why? Because at eighteen, your child graduates from high school and no longer has access to the public education system. In Canada, we have a three-year grace period as the public education system ceases at twenty-one, but the result is the same.

After our children are considered adults, there is little available to them in terms of education, employment, training, health care, housing, and leisure activities. If your child isn't autonomous, is severely autistic, and has an intellectual disability like Nico, he will likely remain at home and lose all the skills acquired during the years of early intervention and school.

This rips at my soul every chance it gets. You see, having lost my identity while taking care of Nico 24/7 for at least nine years, I dread getting caught in the same dark space once again. Hence my sense of urgency. *I have three years to make a difference in this world and to spread my messages of empowerment.*

Claudia Taboada

What's Next?

A. The Burnout to Unstoppable Women's Empowerment Community. Anyone leading a chronically stressful life and want to get their spark back by prioritizing self-care and self-fulfillment? Whether you're a special needs mom, a stay-at-home mom, a mom who is burned out and overwhelmed with work and family responsibilities, or someone who's living a highly stressful life, my heart is with you. I want you to take charge, be the leader of your life, and become the Unstoppable Badass that you're meant to be.

For that, I'll be creating several initiatives in 2020 to mentor and motivate you on your quest for a better YOU:

1. Two more books: *Rediscovering the Unstoppable Badass in You: The Busy Women's Guide to Self-Care, Fitness, Stress Management, and Living Your Best Life* and *Marathons, Maslow, and Mindset: The Life-Transforming Power of Running and How It Helps Me Cope and Thrive.*

2. A private Facebook group where we can support, inspire, and celebrate each other. More details will be given once you join my email list.

3. Online courses on different topics, including stress resilience and building a badass mindset, running as the all encompassing self-care tool and my proprietary method Holistic Self-Care Blueprint for an Unstoppable You.

4. One-on-one transformational life coaching services.

5. Fitness, yoga, & mindset retreats in the beautiful setting of Mont-Tremblant.

B. **The Claudia Taboada Foundation.** In the next couple of years, I'll be starting a foundation to help two populations that have been forgotten by society and governments around the world:

(1) severely autistic adults and their families. Services for the adult autistic population are almost non-existent at the present in the province of Québec, the other Canadian provinces, and most countries around the world. Those adults who are severely autistic with severe communication and behavior issues and with an intellectual disability have even less possibilities of employment, adult learning, and specialized housing. What are the parents of these severely autistic adults to do? Stay home and care for their child all day? Unfortunately, yes. This is the outcome and since the majority of full-time caregivers are mothers, they're the ones who pay the price for the government's lack of inaction. My wish is to encourage the start of a movement of autism warrior caregivers from around the world who will fight tooth and nail for services for their severely autistic children. I have divided these needs into five categories: 1) adult education; 2) employment and training 3) adapted housing 4) adapted leisure activities 5) family support and respite to caregivers. The idea is to advocate for our children and to target government decision makers and business leaders to fund existing or new initiatives.

(2) overwhelmed and burned-out special needs caregivers. My special needs full-time caregiving mommas who are the most prone to burnout and chronic stress have been forgotten by governments and society alike. They have as many rights to self-fulfillment and to living up to their full potential as anybody else. Let's join forces together and help these mommas around the world take a stand and have a voice so they can approach governments and business leaders with confidence to ask for funding and services (e.g., increase in respite services for example) to help them cope and thrive while continuing to care for their children with dignity.

If you have any ideas about how we can help these two populations, contact me directly at badassautismmoma@gmail.com.

C. Tâ_bo Active by Claudia T. Stylish sportswear brand seeking to empower and inspire busy women like you to get active and take care of yourselves – walking, running, gym, yoga, whatever makes you tick but do it with passion and consistency. More details to come.

BE PART OF THE COMMUNITY BY JOINING MY PRIVATE FACEBOOK GROUP

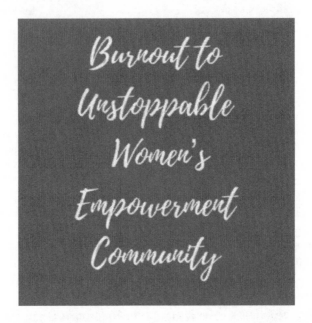

This Private Facebook Group is geared to supporting the readers of my Women Empowerment Book Series. It's for busy, overwhelmed and burned-out women, including special needs moms like myself and moms who are burning the candle at both ends because of family and work responsibilities. It's a safe place where we can connect with each other and learn about self-care, fitness, stress management, and, most importantly, building a strong and resilient mindset that will enable us to go after our dreams fearlessly and with conviction.

It's about taking charge of our lives by prioritizing self-care, rediscovering our spark, and becoming *UNSTOPPABLE*.

This year, my charity of choice will be the Giant Steps Foundation, and I will give a portion of the proceeds of my books to this wonderful organization. The Giant Steps Foundation contributes to the operating costs of the Montreal Giant Steps School for autistic children – Nico's home away from home.

The Giant Steps School and the Giant Steps Foundation

Founded in 1980, the Giant Steps School is a tuition-free private school that welcomes students aged 4 to 21 years old with autism. Educational services are offered in French and English. The vision of the school is to be a leader and hub for the development and provision of services supporting the education and success of people with autism. The Giant Steps Foundation was founded in order to offer financial support to the Giant Steps School. The Giant Steps School relies heavily on the Foundation to raise over $1,000,000 per year for the school.

The Giant Steps Work Placement Program

Adults with autism have some of the poorest employment outcomes in comparison to others with disabilities. More than 80% of people on the autism spectrum are unemployed. Improving employment outcomes is not only important, but also urgent. **Better work opportunities improve quality of life, independence, and social integration.** What individuals with autism need is the right kind of support.

That's why **Giant Steps has created a work placement program** for its teens and young adults (aged 16 to 21). Students are matched with work placements according to **their interests** and are **always accompanied by their specialized educator.** When the pairing is successful, we notice:

- **Increased self-esteem, confidence and self-reliance;**
- **Active participation in community life;**
- **Development of professional skills;**
- **Generalization of skills acquired within the school;**
- **Increased independence and autonomy for all students;**
- **Exploration of interests and work abilities.**

If you're interested in supporting the Foundation, the School and this very important Work Placement Program, you can donate online at: https://interland3.donorperfect.net/weblink /WebLink.aspx?name=giantsteps&id=1

For more information, contact: Tracy Pennimpede, Giant Steps Foundation Director at (514) 935-1911 x 226 or by email at Director Foundation tpennimpede@giantstepsmontreal.com

And here is a peek at the cover of my *SECOND* book in my Women's Empowerment Series which is coming out in late spring:

Rediscovering the Unstoppable Badass in You: The Busy Women's Guide to Self-Care, Fitness, Stress Management, a Badass Mindset, and Living Your Best Life

For **EXCLUSIVE** news about the release of my second book subscribe to
https://www.badassautismmoma.com/Unstoppablebadassbook

About the Author

Claudia Taboada has a B. Sc. in Biochemistry and LL.B. in Common Law from the University of Ottawa. She is a former labor and employment attorney, a disability rights advocate, a multiple marathon finisher and triathlete, an author, an entrepreneur, and a transformational life coach and speaker, living in Montréal. Claudia's most precious and important role is that of being a devoted mom to her two sons Nico and Alex.

The seed for Claudia's passion was planted when seventeen years ago, she decided to abandon her law career to care full time for Nico, who had been newly diagnosed with classic autism. Claudia became her son's teacher, therapist, advocate, specialist, early intervention program manager... In all of this whirlwind, she lost her identity. She was burned out, overwhelmed, depressed, and living life on autopilot. One day, Nico was given a service dog, Sicas, who became Claudia's life savior. She started taking Sicas out for walks. These walks turned into two-minute runs then one-km runs around the block, etc. Running became Claudia's passion and her primary self-care tool.

Slowly but surely, this helped Claudia get her physical, emotional, and mental health back and more. She decided then that she wanted to learn everything about the different self-care tools available and the strategies that she could implement in her daily life to become stress resilient and ward off burnouts, all while parenting her severely autistic son Nico with grace. Claudia then reinvented herself as an endurance athlete, yoga enthusiast, and passionate wellness and self-care advocate with an interest in personal development, self-actualization, stress resilience, and mindset.

Claudia loves hearing from her readers, so you can also contact her directly at badassautismmoma@gmail.com. You can also learn more about her services and reach out to her via her website: https://www.ClaudiaTaboada.com/

Acknowledgements

Thank you to my two boys, Nico and Alex for inspiring and motivating me to be the best person I can be. I wrote this book so that you can be proud of your momma and to show you that *anything is possible* if you put your mind to it.

Thank you to my mom Leticia and to my grandma Conchita who are both watching from heaven. If I can become half the badass that you two were in your lifetimes, I will die content.

Thank you to Rob. Even though we have mutually decided to go our separate ways after 22 years of marriage, I trust that we will continue to co-parent our boys with grace and make our kids an absolute priority. Most importantly, I trust that we will continue to work towards the best future for both our boys, especially Nico's.

Thank you to my writing coach Sloan Ketcham, my editor Katie Chambers of Beacon Point LLC, and my proofreader, formatter and KDP expert Wayne Purdin. Without all of you, I wouldn't have been able to get this book out to the masses.

Thank you to Montréal photographer extraordinaire Yves Lacombe, hair and make-up artist Dany Cournoyer, and artistic director Patrick Craig for the awesome front and back cover photos.

Thank you to my dear friends Stephanie Avakian-Chown for her valuable feedback with regards to the cover layout and for bouncing off ideas about possible titles and subtitles for this book.

To all of the wonderful staff at Nico's home away from home, Montréal's Giant Steps School for autistic children. These miracle workers do their best to nurture their student's talents all while dealing with all sorts of behaviors on a daily basis. The peace of mind provided by this school and its staff enabled me to have the mental clarity and the tranquility to focus and get this book done.

To Sicas for making me discover the joys of running and for literally saving my life.

To my first running coach Pierre Léveillé for his patience and making me believe in my potential. To my current running coach Dorys Langlois for motivating me, challenging me, and helping me become the best runner I can be.

To my runner and triathlete friends, I am grateful for our friendships and for the constant motivation, inspiration and accountability that you provide.

To all of you burned out and overwhelmed special needs mommas around the world, you are the main reason why I wrote this book. Caregiver burnout is a real issue that needs to be taken seriously by society, governments and business leaders everywhere. I hope that I was able to shine a light on this topic and start the conversation.

Finally, thank you to all of you my readers, I hope you enjoyed reading my story as much as I enjoyed writing it. Feel free to reach out to me via email at badassautismmoma@gmail.com. You can also subscribe to the following:

- My business page: https://ClaudiaTaboada.com/
- My autism blog: https://advocatesforautismrights.com/
- My Fitness, Travel, and Wellness Blog: https://www.badassautismmoma.com/

You can also follow me on social media:

- My fitness account on instagram: https://www.instagram.com/badassautismmomma/
- My Business Facebook page: Claudia Taboada, Author and Speaker
- My private Facebook group: The Burnout to Unstoppable Women's Empowerment Community

Help Me Spread My Message

Reviews are key when building excitement and authority for a book. If you read and enjoyed *Burnout to Unstoppable*, I would love it if you could leave your honest review on Amazon, Goodreads, or other relevant websites where you can leave book reviews. This will help me spread my message and start the conversation around the issues of caregiver burnout and the need for us all to become stress resilient and prioritize self-care.

End Notes

[1] Alli, Renée A. "The Types of Autism Spectrum Disorder." *Web MD*, 12 November 2108.
https://www.webmd.com/brain/autism/autism-spectrum-disorders

[2] "Classic Autism." *Medic 8*.
https://www.medic8.com/mental-health/autism/classic-autism.html

[3] Drayden-Edwards Roxanne and Melissa Conrad Stoppler. ''What Are the Symptoms and Signs of Autism.'', *eMedicineHealth*, Web MD L.L.C.
https://www.emedicinehealth.com/autism/article_em.htm#what_are_sympto ms_and_signs_of_autism

[4] Long, Sasha. "Generalization: Take It Away from the Table." *The Autism Helper*, 25 January 2017.
https://theautismhelper.com/generalization-take-away-table/

[5] "Interview with Dr. Stephen Shore: Autism Advocates and on the Spectrum." *IBCCES.org*, International Board of Credentials and Continuing Education Standards, 23 March 2017.
https://ibcces.org/blog/2018/03/23/12748/

[6] Brooke Ingersoll, "The Social Role of Imitation in Autism Implication for the Treatment of Imitation Deficits," *Infants and Young Children,* 2008; vol. 21, no. 2: 107-119.
https://depts.washington.edu/isei/iyc/21.2_Ingersoll.pdf

[7] O'Callaghan, Ellen. "Dr. Temple Grandin: Focus on Strengths Rather Than Deficits in Children with Autism," *Irish Examiner*, 4 August 2017.
https://www.irishexaminer.com/lifestyle/healthandlife/dr-temple-grandin-focus-on-strengths-rather-than-deficits-in-children-with-autism-456215.html

[8] "Talking Readiness (Pre-Language Skills)." Kid Sense Child Development Corporation Pty Ltd.
https://childdevelopment.com.au/areas-of-concern/using-speech/talking-readiness-pre-language-skills/

[9] "Autism Spectrum Disorders: Communication Problems in Children." *National Institute of Deafness and Other Communication Disorders (NIDCD)*, US Department of Health and Human Services.
https://www.nidcd.nih.gov/health/autism-spectrum-disorder-communication-problems-children

[10] Pullen, Lara. "Social Stories," *Autism Canada,* Autism Canada. 11 December 2017.
https://autismcanada.org/living-with-autism/treatments/non-medical/communication/social-stories/

[11] "How Does School Shadowing Help a Child with ASD Succeed in School." *Stepping Stones*, Stepping Stones Center. 4 October 2016.

https://www.steppingstonesca.com/single-post/2016/10/25/How-does-school-shadowing-help-a-child-with-ASD-succeed-in-school

[12] "Conditions Comorbid to Autism Spectrum Disorders," *Wikipedia*, 7 September 2019. https://en.wikipedia.org/wiki/Conditions_comorbid_to_autism_spectrum_di sorders#Comorbid_conditions

[13] "ADHD or Autism," *Web MD*, Web MD L.L.C. https://www.webmd.com/add-adhd/childhood-adhd/adhd-or-autism#1

[14] "Self-Injurious Behaviour," *National Autistic Society*, October 2016. https://www.autism.org.uk/about/behaviour/challenging-behaviour/self-injury.aspx

[15] "Epilepsy," *Mayo Clinic*, Mayo Foundation for Medical Education and Research (MFMER), 27 November 2018. https://www.mayoclinic.org/diseases-conditions/epilepsy/symptoms-causes/syc-20350093

[16] Gutstein, Steve. "Foundations of Dynamic Intelligence, Episode #69," *RDI Connect*, 13 September 2019. https://www.rdiconnect.com/foundations-of-dynamic-intelligence-episode-69/

[17] Rudacille, Deborah. "IQ Scores Not a Good Measure of Function in Autism," *Spectrum* , Simons Foundation, 6 January 2011. https://www.spectrumnews.org/news/iq-scores-not-a-good-measure-of-function-in-autism/

[18] Tony Charman et al., "IQ in Children with Autism Spectrum Disorders: Data from the Special Needs and Autism Spectrum Disorder," *Psychol Med* 2011 March 4 1(3): 619-27. https://www.ncbi.nlm.nih.gov/pubmed/21272389

[19] Vasilopoulou E. et al. "The Quality of Life of Parents of Children with Autism Spectrum Disorder: A Systematic Review," *Research in Autism Spectrum Disorders*, Volume 23, March 2016: 36-49. https://www.sciencedirect.com/science/article/pii/S1750946715300064

[20] Zablotsky B et al. "The Association Between Child Autism Symptomology, Maternal Quality of Life and Risk for Depression," *J Autism Dev Disord.* 2013; vol. 43, no. 8: 1946-1955. https://www.ncbi.nlm.nih.gov/pubmed/23263770

[21] Bonis S. "Stress and Parents of Children with Autism: A Review of Literature," *Issues Ment Health Nurs.* 2016; vol. 37, no. 3: 153-163. https://www.ncbi.nlm.nih.gov/pubmed/27028741

[22] Miodrag N, Hodapp RM. "Chronic Stress and Health Among Parents of Children with Intellectual Disabilities," *Opin Psychiatry.* 2010; vol. 23, no. 5: 407-411. https://www.ncbi.nlm.nih.gov/pubmed/20592593

[23] Epel E., Blackburn E. et al. "Accelerated Telomere Shortening in Response to Life Stress," *Proc Natl Acad Sci USA.* 2004 Dec 7; vol. 101, no. 49: 17312-5.

https://www.ncbi.nlm.nih.gov/pubmed/15574496

[24] Diament, Michelle. "Autism Moms Have Stress Similar to Combat Soldiers." *Disability Scoop*, LLC. 10 November, 2009.
https://www.disabilityscoop.com/2009/11/10/autism-moms-stress/6121/

[25] Smith L.E., Mailik Seltzer M. et al, "Daily Experiences Among Mothers of Adolescents and Adults with Autism Spectrum Disorder," *J Autism Dev Disord*. 2010 Feb; vol. 40, no. 2: 167-78.
https://www.ncbi.nlm.nih.gov/pubmed/19655239

[26] Mailik Seltzer M. et al. "Maternal Cortisol Levels and Behaviour Problems in Adolescents and Adults with ASD," *J Autism Dev Disord* 2010 Apr. vol. 40, no. 4: 457-469.
https://www.ncbi.nlm.nih.gov/pmc/articles/PMC2837763/

[27] "Challenging Behaviour in Children and Teenagers with Autism Spectrum," Raising Children Network (Australia) Limited.
https://raisingchildren.net.au/autism/behaviour/understanding-behaviour/challenging-behaviour-asd

[28] Fischbach, R. L. et al. "Understanding the Experience of Stigma for Parents of Children with Autism Spectrum Disorder and the Role Stigma Plays in Families' Lives." *J Autism Dev Disord*. 2015.
https://www.ncbi.nlm.nih.gov/pubmed/?term=Kinnear+SH%2C+Link+BG%2C+Ballan+MS%2C+Fischbach+RL

[29] Furfaro, Hannah. "Sleep Problems in Autism Explained." *Spectrum*, Simons Foundation, 13 November 2017.
https://www.spectrumnews.org/news/sleep-problems-autism-explained/

[30] Johnson KP, Malow BA "Sleep in Children with Autism Spectrum Disorders." *Curr Treat Options Neurol*. 2008; vol. 10, no. 5: 350-9
https://www.ncbi.nlm.nih.gov/pubmed/18782508

[31] Doo, Sylvia and Kwok Wing, Yu. "Sleep Problems of Children with Pervasive Development Disorders: Correlation with Parental Stress." *Developmental Medicine and Child Neurology*, August 2006; vol. 48, no. 8: 650-655. Published by Cambridge University Press: 12 July 2006.
https://doi.org/10.1017/S001216220600137X

[32] Baker DL, Drapela LA. "Mostly the Mother: Concentration of Adverse Employment Effects on Mothers of Children with Autism." The Social Science Journal. 2010; vol. 47, no. 3: 578-592.
https://www.sciencedirect.com/science/article/abs/pii/S0362331910000169

[33] Ouellete, Gabriel et al. "Rapport de Recherche: Les Parents des Enfants Autistes Ont-ils Les Outils Nécessaires pour Concilier Travail et Famille." 10 mars 2017.
https://www.autisme.qc.ca/assets/files/02-autisme-tsa/Recherche/Rapport_BIM720_autisme_final.pdf

[34] Cidav Z. et al. "Implications of Childhood Autism for Parental Employment and Earnings." *Pediatrics*. 2012; vol. 129, no. 4: 617-23.
https://www.ncbi.nlm.nih.gov/pubmed/22430453

[35] "Autism Facts and Figures." *Autism Speaks*

https://www.autismspeaks.org/autism-facts-and-figures

[36] Ibid.

[37] Parish S.L. "Juggling and Struggling: A Preliminary Work-Life Study of Mothers with Adolescents who Have Developmental Disabilities." *Ment Retard*. 2006; vol. 44, no. 6: 393-404. https://www.ncbi.nlm.nih.gov/pubmed/17132034

[38] Fernandez-Alcantara M. et al. "Feelings of Loss and Grief in Parents of Children Diagnosed with Autism Spectrum Disorder (ASD)." *Research in Developmental Disabilities*. August 2016; vol 55: 312-321. https://www.ncbi.nlm.nih.gov/pubmed/27235768

[39] Michael, Raphailia. "What Self-Care Is and What Self-Care Isn't." *PsychCentral*, 8 July 2017

[40] "Self-care." *Oxford Dictionary*.

[41] McLeod, Saul. "Maslow's Hierarchy of Needs," *Simply Psychology*, Creative Commons, 21 May 2018. https://www.simplypsychology.org/maslow.html

[42] "Physical Activity Reduces Stress," *Anxiety and Depression Association of America*, ADAA. https://adaa.org/understanding-anxiety/related-illnesses/other-related-conditions/stress/physical-activity-reduces-st

[43] Mayo Clinic Staff, "Exercise and Stress: Get Moving to Manage Stress." *Mayo Clinic*, Mayo Foundation For Medical Education and Research (MFFMER), https://www.mayoclinic.org/healthy-lifestyle/stress-management/in-depth/exercise-and-stress/art-20044469

[44] Lavelle, Julie. "New Brain Effects Behind Runners High," *Scientific American*, 8 October 2015 https://www.scientificamerican.com/article/new-brain-effects-behind-runner-s-high/

[45] Fetters, Alicia. "How to Achieve a Runner's High," *Runner's World*, 11 August 2019 https://www.runnersworld.com/training/a20851505/how-to-achieve-a-runners-high/

[46] Craft, L.L. et al. "The Benefits of Exercise for the Clinically Depressed," *Prim Care Companion J Clin Psychiatry*, 2004; vol. 6, no. 3: 104-111; https://www.ncbi.nlm.nih.gov/pmc/articles/PMC474733/

[47] "Exercise for Stress and Anxiety." *Anxiety and Depression Association of America*, ADAA. https://adaa.org/living-with-anxiety/managing-anxiety/exercise-stress-and-anxiety

[48] "Mindfulness." *Oxford Dictionary*.

[49] "What Is Mindfulness," *Greater Good Magazine*, The Greater Good Science Center at the University of Berkley, California, https://greatergood.berkeley.edu/topic/mindfulness/definition

[50] "Benefits of Mindfulness," *HelpGuide*. Adapted with permission from *Positive Psychology: Harnessing the Power of Happiness, Personal Strength,*

and Mindfulness, a special health report published by Harvard Health Publishing.
https://www.helpguide.org/harvard/benefits-of-mindfulness.htm
[51] "Journaling for Mental Health," *Health Encyclopedia,* University of Rochester Medical Center, Rochester
https://www.urmc.rochester.edu/encyclopedia/content.aspx?ContentID=4552&ContentTypeID=1
[52] Scott, Elizabeth. "The Benefits of Journaling for Stress Management," *Verywellmind*, 23 October, 2019,
https://www.verywellmind.com/the-benefits-of-journaling-for-stress-management-3144611
[53] Robinson Mayer, Kara. "How Writing in a Journal Helps to Manage Depression" *WebMD*.
https://www.webmd.com/depression/features/writing-your-way-out-of-depression#1
[54] Carr, K. *Crazy Sexy Diet*. Guilford, CT: Skirt! 2011.
[55] Atasoy, Ozgun. "Your Thoughts Can Release Abilities Beyond Normal Limits," *ScientificAmerican.com*, 13 August 2013
https://www.scientificamerican.com/article/your-thoughts-can-release-abilities-beyond-normal-limits/
[56] Pawlowski, A. "Feeling Stressed: How to Change Mindset for a Better Day," *Today.com*, NBC Universal, 19 January 2018
https://www.today.com/health/positive-stress-mindset-helps-people-perform-busy-day-t121370
[57] Jaret, Peter. "The Surprising Benefits of Stress." *University of California Berkley's Greater Good Magazine*, 20 October 2015,
https://greatergood.berkeley.edu/article/item/the_surprising_benefits_of_stress
[58] Collier, Lorna. "Growth After Trauma, Why Are Some People More Resilient Than Others and Can It Be Taught?" *American Psychology Association*, November 2016,
https://www.apa.org/monitor/2016/11/growth-trauma
[59] "Center for Expertise in Autism," *SACCADE Centre d'Expertise en Autisme*, SACCADE.
https://saccade.ca/english.php
[60] Harrisson, Brigitte and St-Charles, Lise. *New Ways of Understanding Autism*. Dondrum, 2019.
[61] Grandin, Temple. *Thinking in Pictures: My Life with Autism*. New York, NY: Vintage; 2008.
[62] Grandin, Temple. *Different...Not Less: Inspiring Stories of Achievement and Successful Employment from Adults with Autism, Asperger's and ADHD*. Arlington, TX: Future Horizons, 2012
[63] O'Callaghan, Ellen. "Dr. Temple Grandin: Focus on Strengths Rather Than Deficits in Children with Autism," *Irish Examiner*, 4 August 2017.

https://www.irishexaminer.com/lifestyle/healthandlife/dr-temple-grandin-focus-on-strengths-rather-than-deficits-in-children-with-autism-456215.html
[64] Bashore, Mark. "Interview: Scientist/Inventor Temple Grandin on the Potential of People on the Autism Spectrum." *WKarNews*, 23 November 2016.
https://www.wkar.org/post/scientistinventor-temple-grandin-potential-people-autism-spectrum#stream/0

Made in the USA
San Bernardino, CA
10 February 2020

64245096R00136